IS YOUR BUSINESS RIGHT FOR FRANCHISING?

IS YOUR BUSINESS RIGHT FOR FRANCHISING?

Ralph Massetti Jr

Is Your Business Right For Franchising?

Author: Ralph J. Massetti, Jr. - President & CEO

The Franchise Builders | www.thefranchisebuilders.com

Publisher: LuLu.com | c/o The Franchise Builders | www.thefranchisebuilders.com

Book design by Josh McCowen

IBSN #: 978-1-4303-1559-9

dedication

This book is lovingly dedicated to the two Mothers in my life.

First, to my Mother, who is unable to be here and witness the achievements of her hard work in me. She was a true example of what the power of love and belief in others can achieve, and I am eternally grateful for the gifts that having her as a Mother would unknowingly give me. She is truly missed and I am challenged everyday to love as deeply as she had.

Secondly, to the love of my life, soul mate and Mother to my wonderful children, Kim. She has been an endless source of inspiration, and a giver of unconditional love and commitment, even when it meant her own self-sacrifice. She has singularly defined for me and our family what it means to be courageous and we are blessed to have her in our lives. I still cherish each moment with her as if it where my first and look excitedly forward to a life filled with love and joy with her at my side.

Lastly, my dedication would not be complete without the thanks and expression of love to my remaining family and children, all of which make my life meaningful. Each fill a special place in my heart and I am hopeful that I lovingly "give back" in the way that I receive.

acknowledgments

This work is the result of a series of events and experiences that brought me to this moment. Consequently, there are many whose contributions allow me the knowledge to contribute to the franchise industry in what I am hopeful proves to be a materially, meaningful way.

This list includes memorable instructors and educators, co-workers and numerous gifted employees, unselfish vendors and personally available clients, all of whom my gratitude and appreciation is expressed.

Specifically, I send thanks to my current team of dedicated employees, who make my work not only worthwhile, but entertaining. I witness their personal commitment to my company and our clients every day, and their work not only inspires me, but simply makes me proud. My goal is to create a company that not only rewards them and their families generously, but returns the pride that I share.

Also, my acknowledgments would not be complete without the thanks of my clients, of whom most have become my personal friends. I am grateful for the opportunity to work with each of you and witness the rewards that great work has bestowed on your businesses. And, I am equally appreciative of the shared experiences that each of your businesses have contributed to my body of knowledge.

Lastly, special thanks to Rob Hanson of Garage Floor Coating for allowing the public publication of his franchise's Uniform Franchise Offering Circular in the Exhibit section.

contents

INTRODUCTION

CONCLUSION

APPENDIX A

ABOUT THE AUTHOR

INTRODUCTION

Good Day! If I were to meet you in person, I would predictably say, hello...I am Ralph Massetti! Then, odds are we would have a short discussion and laugh about how my surname sounds like the knife "Machete", or that I look like Ralph Malph from Happy Days with the red hair and all. And that is okay; I am used to it and embrace my uniqueness. As we spoke further, I'd likely share that I am a Midwestern Irish/Italian, born and raised in the city of Chicago, and currently dividing my home life between residences in Phoenix, Denver and Tampa, FL. Barring, the personal experience, I wanted to paint a personal picture of myself for this introduction and forewarn you that I intended to write this book and cover this content from a specifically unique voice.

My goal is to speak plainly and frankly about the industry of franchising in the hopes that this learning exercise proves to be a rewarding and honest experience as you gather facts and figures about the prospect of franchising your business. Fact is, I too have read the majority of the books and likely surfed the same Websites that you have, and I am concerned about the "sameness" of the information presented, and the lack of perspective and genuine disclosure about becoming a Franchisor today.

Additionally, I have spoken directly, and noted from hundreds of my clients and prospects, common similarities in what is being told to would-be Franchisors by legitimate and so-called professional franchise industry development experts. This group includes Franchise Attorneys and formal Franchise Consultants and Developers (of which my business is defined).

Frankly, in my opinion, many and most of these experts are either knowingly or unknowingly misleading business people considering franchising. This misleading information varies in their deliberation and severity, but nevertheless are common. Many service providers commit a common offense by over-stating the ultimate importance on only the portion of the development process that they perform, such as Legal Document Drafting.

For example, there are countless franchise developers and lawyers that, like a broken record, tell prospects that the "most critical" part of the franchise development process is the Uniform Franchise Offering Circular (UFOC) and Franchise Agreement, and that they should spend the majority of their time (and coincidentally, their money) on drafting these documents.

Now, while I agree that these documents are vital and that their preparation needs to be facilitated by competent legal counsel, they are far from all that is "critical" to a Franchisor's success, and only the beginning of what is required to develop a well-crafted franchise organization capable of achieving notable growth.

I am not suggesting that all the professionals that service the Franchisor are intentionally misleading their prospects and clients. I am merely suggesting that franchising is like any other business. It requires the right blend of operational expertise, marketing and branding uniqueness, product innovation and differentiation, trademark evidence, legal and financial preparedness and proper funding. All too often, I am meeting new Franchisors that have spent upwards of $125,000 for two legal documents that are largely the same required legal "boilerplate" and then told by their legal and development professionals that they are ready to "go sell". With that, the new Franchisor goes to the marketplace with a mediocre branding and identity, a largely unplanned operational system, a poorly prepared franchise manual and no real preparation of what it is really going to be like to be a Franchisor.

If you were to call my business, The Franchise Builders, and ask for information about franchising your business, you would, in almost every case, share a lengthy conversation with me. As there is no "official" franchise industry licensing, talking to me would be more a measure of faith of my competence, likely gained by your review of my company's Website, or from a recommendation from one of our clients.

That aside, I would ask you several specific questions about your current business and with that, we would start a hearty and blunt conversation about whether I (and you) felt your business had the merit, model and multiplicity factor needed to make it a successful franchise offering. Odds are, and this is where I differ from most "franchise consulting experts", that your business would not be one that I would recommend you making the investment required to formally franchise. In any case, it is likely we would end on a positive note, with a future plan of action to prepare your business for franchising at a later date, your finding a renewed resolve in continuing with your current business structure and avoiding franchising, or our continuing our conversation by further exploring the factors and costs of immediately franchising your business.

Rest assured, although I may frequent a critical stand in this book, I love franchising. I am appreciative of the reward and fulfillment it has provided me and my family, and I am blessed to have made some lasting friendships among my clients. Furthermore, I am a frequent witness to the financial reward and the magnitude and effect of franchising's power of multiplicity that my clients have enjoyed.

I am hopeful that the information you gain from this book will prove rewarding for you and your business, should you decide to venture into franchising or seek an alternate expansion method. I would like nothing more than to hear of your success personally and as an entrepreneur myself, I have the highest level of admiration for the effort and commitment required to build a world-class business organization worthy of selling to others.

So, with an MBA, a comprehensive amount of franchise

marketing and development experience and an impressive list of satisfied franchise clients, I set out to provide you the same consultation experience, minus your participation of course, and provide you the opportunity to explore franchising for your business with certainty and finality.

CHAPTER 1

The Big Question

are you ready?

Is my business ready for franchising? This is the most common question that we receive at The Franchise Builders on initial calls with potential Franchisors. In fact, when most Franchisors calls us for the first time, that is all they really want to know; whether we too agree that their business is ready to benefit from a franchise model for expansion.

Similarly, I begin our first conversation with the same goal and we proceed with the qualification process by my asking a series of questions to make this determination. We will discuss topics such as how long the business has been operating, where the business is located, whether the business has moved or has ever operated in other geographic areas, whether it is considered a "local" favorite, and more importantly, what is considered the most compelling differentiators that make the business competitively effective against other businesses in the area and the same industry.

Additionally, we would explore what the expectations were for the long-term success of the business, and discuss whether it is probable that the business could maintain its success perpetually, or is susceptible to certain industry, competitive, regulatory, cyclical, or other external or internal threats. Oftentimes, business owners will refer to industry shifts, regulatory challenges or market maturity issues for fueling their desire to franchise their business and shift its growth and risk to external parties. Too often, when owners know or sense that their business is in decline, they look to franchising as either a last-ditch effort to continue their businesses expansion, or as an exit strategy, facilitated by third-party investment.

On the other hand, many businesses are doing terrifically well and the owner is looking for options to expand their business without being directly tied to the day-to-day operational requirements and/or having to personally fund the expansion effort. Put simply, some owners have done an outstanding job building exceedingly successful businesses, but are simply "burned out" from the repetition of the operational aspects of operating their business. Further, they are looking for retirement and wealth creation beyond what is possible by their direct work efforts at the business' current location(s). These are among the best franchise prospects.

an ideal franchise candidate

Businesses that benefit from consistent, local success with a qualified, albeit exhausted owner, also enjoy a great probability of success in franchising. For example, I spoke with a potential client who owned a Catfish Restaurant in Arkansas. Admittedly, I didn't know what to expect when I initiated the conversation, and I was pleasantly surprised by his business success.

Essentially, his business was a local favorite for delicious, "home cooked" fried catfish, fried chicken and barbecue ribs, along with one-of-a-kind and perfectly crafted southern side dishes. This gentleman had been in the business for over thirty years now and his 300-seat restaurant in a small town in Arkansas reportedly serves over 750 diners a day, while open only twenty hours a week. He further shared that many of his customers openly share the fact that they had just got off a plane or completed a 100-mile drive to eat at his restaurant. This kind of customer loyalty and demand creates the strongest brands and long-term success stories. He has undoubtedly not only appealed to the locals, but has made loyal customers of residents from essentially every state in the nation after having happened upon his restaurant at some point in the last thirty years.

8

When I asked him why he wanted to expand into franchising for his business, I was certain how he would reply. His motivations were very simple and he admitted that after running his business for over thirty years, helping prepare over eighty pounds of catfish every day, and running all the operational aspects of the restaurant, he had simply had enough.

note Business owners frequently explore franchising as means to exit the daily operations of their business, and focus on more strategic growth objectives.

Consequently, even though his business, an extremely successful enterprise earning over two million dollars a year with only one small location, was doing well, he was looking for an exit strategy from the day-to-day operations. He also wanted to not only distribute his product to a larger market, but more importantly, have others make the investment and the operational commitment to do so.

Additionally, the issues that would need to be addressed for him to expand his business personally with any great significance simply presented themselves to him as excessive and exhausting. This scenario is an ideal example of a franchise prospect. One that has a business that has been largely successful and has enjoyed many years of consistent growth and profitability, has survived a number of business cyclical cycles, including recessions, expansions, demographics shifts and more, yet has managed to not only maintain a loyal customers base, but has also been able to earn considerable profitability despite changing eating habits, differing tastes, fluctuating dietary trends and increasing competition.

the other half

Unfortunately, the large majority of my initial calls with prospective Franchisors aren't quite as exciting as the one described above. The fact is, we regularly receive calls from business owners that have no reason to consider franchising their business, and many start by immediately asserting the fact that their business is either, new, struggling, or not even opened yet, but that they think their current or future business will be the next great American franchise.

tip Unfortunately, the vast majority of businesses are not, at least initially, prepared and/or qualified to benefit from franchising.

Because franchising is consistently reported as being such a hot industry, it tends to give the impression to would-be Franchisors that it is much, much simpler than it sounds to become a franchise powerhouse, and many equate the "build it and they will come" mentality with the franchise industry. It is quite concerning how many business owners and opportunists assume that any business can be easily franchised and replicated by the hundreds into successful units.

The most shocking are the prospects that call with an idea, a concept, or reference an industry that they think might be experiencing high growth and that they want to start both their first location and the development of their franchise simultaneously. Some don't have an interest in opening even one location, instead they take confidence in their business wisdom to create a winning operational and competitive business conceptually, and expect Franchisees to come calling to buy their share of the magic. Imagine being a franchise prospect and being solicited for a franchise that

10

has either no locations or only recently began in business.

The sad truth is there are numerous operators doing just that. And while, I am not suggesting that it is impossible to do this, particularly in established industries, it is more likely that unless the originating business owner is a superb business strategist, the model and the franchise will not flourish and will likely suffer from the same dangers that threaten all businesses. Additionally, prematurely developed and occasional fraudulent franchise development has largely led to most of the current franchise legislation and regulations Franchisors are forced to navigate today.

franchise fees are not the reason to franchise

In my opinion, the temptation to prematurely or undeservingly develop a franchise is largely caused by one flaw in thinking. Put simply, that making money in franchising is just about selling franchises. When consulting my company's prospects, I am quick to point out that selling franchises and the revenue received from the initial franchise fees is a zero-sum game. In the end, the costs and responsibilities put on a Franchisor are extensive, and the franchise fees, although significant, generally only provide marginal profit to the Franchisor executing the start-up tasks and other requirements necessary to assist a new owner in the establishment of a franchise location.

Franchise profits, the kind of profits that make franchising a financial windfall for the owner(s), are derived from an annuity stream of on-going franchise royalty payments generated by your Franchisees' success. There is simply no substitution for profitability in a franchise model. Without a long-term cash flow source, a Franchisor will quickly find they are short on capital following a hopeful franchise unit sales run-up. As with any business, franchises experience growth plateaus and maturity points, and franchises need constant royalty cash flow to survive and prosper. The failure of a franchise to provide its units with a quality product or service that is in high demand and will steadily generate royalties, will ultimately mean failure for a franchise network and the Franchisor.

So, if your business sounds more like the Catfish Purveyor, then it is likely franchising can provide you with the means to accomplish significant growth and substantial profits. On the other hand, if your business is new, unproven or now struggling, it is wise to develop an action plan and consider franchising at a later date, or consider another means for expanding your business.

To help decide, you are not alone. I have prepared the next chapter specially to provide a detailed discussion to help you determine the best expansion method for your business today.

12

CHAPTER 2

Expanding Your Business

Franchising is only one of many business expansion alternatives. And, despite the fact that franchising has become such a common expansion method in the United States and abroad, one must still compare and contrast all the available expansion methods available to a business before settling on franchising as the method of choice.

As we have already discussed, franchising is defined as a means of expanding a business by granting a legal license for a third party (Franchisee) to operate a business, limited to a specific operating system and marketing plan, while using the company (Franchisor) trade name, and service mark(s). I restate this definition to refresh your recollection, because as we discuss the other expansion options available to you and your business, it is important that you can recall this specific definition.

maintaining & growing the company store

One obvious choice for the future of your business is to make the choice to maintain your current business course and focus solely on your current existing business location(s). Although this may not be the right decision and it is openly the least dramatic, there are benefits to staying the course.

First, the cost and time commitment required in franchising a business can be excessive, with the costs totaling in excess of one hundred thousand dollars, and in some cases, taking over a year to complete. While there are certainly many methods available to cut costs and save time, by no means is the franchise development process an inexpensive, quick process to complete.

Secondly, becoming a Franchisor requires a significant shift in your current managerial functions. This means that you will no longer be the "owner-operator" of a private, local business. You will quickly transform your daily role into the role of the "the

Franchisor", which requires the use of an entirely new skill set and an abandonment of your current role in the business. While this can be a welcome change for many would-be Franchisors, many find themselves unprepared for the sudden role change and find it difficult to "let go" of their current business operations.

Similarly, many owners are so vital to the success of their business that shifting their focus to the franchising process can prove threatening to the success of the original business location(s).

New Franchisors must firmly believe that taking on a more "executive" approach to their business and focusing on the management of a large, geographically distributed group of Franchisees, is more appealing than the routine operating responsibilities of their current business. Once the commitment is made to franchise, you will be forced to either stay the course as "Franchisor" or hire an experienced executive to manage the growth of your franchise so you can return to the daily management of your original business.

beware   For many new Franchisors, leaving the daily business operations to focus on the growth of their franchise proves their most challenging new responsibility.

Being an entrepreneur most of my life, I feel this point could be among the most significant factors for a business owner considering franchising. When I speak personally to each of my potential clients, I make it a point to visualize this aspect by asserting to them that they must be willing to "walk away" from their current way of doing business, and that they will largely no longer be materially involved in their business as they have been accustomed.

Further, I ask each of them to imagine never returning to

their store, restaurant or other business and greeting customers, vendors and employees again in the same way. I ask them to imagine their current location(s), one day becoming a franchise unit itself, which is often the case, and further assert their future as being limited to being a Franchisor. Not a pizza vendor, childcare service provider, dry cleaner operator or other business owner. Then I ask them again if they think franchising is right for them and their future happiness.

With this notion in mind, we will discuss this issue in more detail in the next chapter, "What to Expect as a Franchisor".

expanding on your own

With the company store doing well, and the desire to expand your business, you will likely consider self-expansion as your initial method for growth. It only makes sense, as your managing and funding the growth of your business puts you in complete control, and makes you the primary benefactor of the value increases along the way.

Expanding on your own, however, has its dark side. First, you and you alone (or with secured or equity shared capital) will have to fund the entire costs of expansion. Depending on your business model, expanding by only a few units could amount to millions of dollars of new capital investment. Further, expansion urges usually come at a time when owners are just beginning to feel the positive cash flow effects of their successful ventures, so facing the prospect of significant reinvestment and sacrifice cannot come at a worse time.

Aside from the capital expense, let us not disregard the challenges associated with recruiting, hiring, training and retaining high quality management and staff to operate the additional locations developed. Remember, in most cases, there is only one owner, and taking on any material expansion strategy of your own means that you are going to be faced with the senior management and operational aspects associated with each location. Your ability to hire and keep good employees will be critical to your self-expansion success and if doing so is outside your normal comfort zone, then it is recommended that you either defer this skill to another executive, or select an alternate expansion method.

With money and management discussed, there still remains a fairly daunting list of tasks and responsibilities facing the owner that chooses to expand independently. They include, site selection and real estate or lease negotiation and financing, general administration, public relations, advertising and crisis management. As each location is being developed and comes on-line, the time commitment and task list will grow accordingly for the owner.

As you can see, considering the money, time and risks, self-expansion is a significant achievement for any business owner. Franchising, by contrast, enables owners to leverage the capital and time resources of their franchise "owners" and thereby expand their brand while mitigating the total risks to their capital, their current business assets and their calendars.

18

the "other" expansion alternatives

I have the word "other" in quotes to intentionally group the remaining options for clarity and sarcasm. Clarity to describe the category, and sarcasm to poke fun at the many expansion methods I am repeatedly presented with, intended to be sly alternatives to traditional franchise development.

As expected, because of the financial, legal and time commitments associated with franchising, business owners frequently look for other methods of expansion that closely approximate the franchise model without failing (knowing or unknowingly) the FTC's franchise definition test in order to avoid complying with the federal and state requirements for franchising. Further, in the majority of these cases, the owner has in fact, developed and is distributing a "franchise", all the while incorrectly insisting that their business is NOT a franchise and they are not obligated to comply with franchise distribution law(s). As expected, most are not happy hearing that they are a sitting duck for a franchise law violation(s) and the target of possible criminal and/or civil charges and damages.

beware Business expansion through franchising should always be considered equally among the remaining expansion methods and never as an impulsive means to an end.

19

The methods referred to take many forms, however, the most common include dealership, distributorship, partnership and limited partnership, joint venture, association and licensor. While each of these expansion methods do have their place, and may in fact, be the best choice for your business, the caution comes in selecting one of the above and the subsequently creating a "franchise" model through the final execution of the model specifics. Specifically, a business is legally defined as a franchise if it meets the following three tests:

1. Allows the buyer to use your company name or logo;

2. Charges a fee to the buyer (inside or outside of product or service);

3. Provides any significant assistance or maintains any significant control over any part of the business.

Clearly, these testing statements are broad in scope, and it is easy to see how difficult it is to expand your business, through outside investment, without failing to affirm the three simple tests above. Owners frequently either make the mistake of developing a franchise model without their knowledge of the law, or intentionally design a system "on the fence" of these franchise litmus tests, often times failing them, when a close examination of the business model is performed. Looking at each expansion alternative more closely, we can quickly conclude the material advantages and disadvantages of each.

dealership, distributorship and licensor

The structure of Dealership and Distributorship expansion options generally limits their use to businesses that manufacture or distribute a physical product. Licensor options can be applied to both service and product business types. Both structures consist of a shared agreement of compromises, as the ability to unilaterally control all agreement options is limited exclusively to franchise agreements. For this reason, you have to be prepared to engage in a relationship with little control over what happens to your product, or how your service is executed once it resides under the control of the dealer, distributor or licensor. The advantage to these expansion options are the speed to market, and limited legal complexities; however, the tendency to impose control or provide material support will likely push these models into the definition of a franchise very easily.

Further, with all expansion alternatives, the allowed use of your trademark is a further qualifier to the franchise test rules. So, if you are considering any expansion alternative to franchising that closely breaches the fringes of the three tests listed above, including the option to use your registered (or otherwise protected)

20

trademarks in a contract relationship, it will likely ensure your business is unwillingly, yet legally, considered a franchise.

partnership, limited partnership and joint venture

Partnerships, Limited Partnerships and Joint Ventures are also an extremely limited expansion method, as is required in order to avoid the auspices of franchise law, the partner(s) must own control to "all" of the units or locations. By contracting with numerous owners for control in one or more, but not all units, it is essentially certain that government agencies will find sufficient evidence to find a franchise law violation. This is particularly true if a shared trademark is involved in the agreement rights. Again, like dealer, distributor and license agreements, partnership agreements are relatively simple to construct, but a long shot in an effort to avoid franchise law and compliance requirements in most realistic expansion executions.

association

Creating an expansion system through an Association structure is considered the most difficult to allow yourself any material benefit, beyond a loose affiliation. The definition of the association system limits control by its nature of very loose contractual agreements. This method, executed properly, can safely avoid the franchise law tests, however, it will likely offer you little or no control on who, how or when your product or service is marketed by the association member(s). This lack of material control and market impact on the expanded system offers no material benefit in most business cases, and should be avoided by all but the most liberally supervised product or service companies.

conclusion

If you are fortunate enough to have developed a business that is worthy of deliberate significant expansion, that is cause enough to celebrate. However, expanding improperly, without proper legal representation or without clear intention, will not only put your existing business at risk, but can also victimize your growth if the wrong expansion vehicle is utilized.

Whether you choose to franchise, or not, be certain of the reasons and associated risks for each expansion option. Franchising, although superior in many cases, is not always the best expansion choice. Many times, your objectives can be met using significantly less expensive and far less complicated agreements. Similarly, when franchising is the best or necessary choice for expanding your business, trying to skirt the legal and regulatory requirements will likely only delay your having to franchise in the end, and can expose you, your business and your investors to unnecessary risks and legal complications.

The best way to determine the best course of action for your business is to consult with competent, reputable consultants and/or attorneys with a strong operational and business acumen.

22

CHAPTER 3

What to Expect as a Franchisor

get ready for a new nine to five

Becoming a Franchisor will be a completely unique experience in contrast to managing your current business, and once your business is franchised, you will immediately be urged to all but abandon your current role in operating your current business, and focus your attention exclusively on the responsibilities required to develop your franchise.

For some owners, this is a welcome change, and possibly the one factor that urged them to considering franchising in the first place. For some, this paradigm shift in their business life becomes a reluctant challenge met with anxiety and reluctance. The fact is most owners have spent extensive years doing only one thing; running their businesses on a daily basis. All too quickly, new Franchisors are forced to shift this responsibility to a qualified manager and focus primarily on their immediate and future franchise development and the continued success of the franchise network.

In doing this, daily business operational tasks are replaced by an emphasis on managerial and strategic focus areas, such as ensuring profitability, maintaining competitive differentiation, Franchisee marketing support, system-wide quality-control, franchise territory development, settling territory disputes, managing trademark issues and more. These tasks rapidly become part of the everyday business life as a Franchisor, and typically, when I initially speak to prospective Franchisors, it becomes immediately clear to me which ones will appreciate and adapt to the new role as being a Franchisor, and which ones will likely reject it.

For instance, I once talked with a prospective franchise client who owned a successful Pizzeria. As we talked, he described in exacting detail what it is like when he interacts with his Pizzeria patrons, how much he enjoys running his daily business and the satisfaction he gets from making great Pizza Pies. Furthermore, he anxiously described the rewards he has enjoyed from watching his business grow and witnessing generations of family members frequent his Pizzeria.

note For some business owners, a deep, sincere love for their current business, can prove to be strong reasoning against franchising.

It only took a few minutes talking to this man to become convinced that he truly loves the business of making pizza. In fact, not once during our talk did he mention the desire to make more money, to eliminate his competition, or to surpass the well-known national brands; things that I often hear first when talking with other would-be Franchisors. He appeared blissfully content with the fulfillment that he is humbly deriving on a daily basis in his Pizzeria.

26

Now, that is not to say that he wouldn't make a capable and successful Franchisor, and even grow to prefer performing the new tasks required as a Franchisor. But, it is urged to anyone who loves operating their business as much as he did to take pause and consider the required changes and what that would mean to their satisfaction and personal fulfillment.

In contrast, consider another potential Franchisor's viewpoint concerning the shift from business owner to Franchisor, and evaluate his welcoming and likely succeeding in the transition. This business owner was the owner of eight wireless telephone retail stores. He had personally funded, opened and staffed each location and was understandably spread thin trying to oversee the operation of these numerous locations.

When he and I initially spoke, he openly shared his desire to aggressively grow his brand, and was honest about his inability to effectively grow the chain beyond its current size without significant personal financial risk and a significant impact on his quality of life and family time. Furthermore, he was excited about the opportunity to shift his business responsibilities to tasks with greater impact and those that can pay returns exponentially as compared to the everyday management tasks of retail store management.

Upon further examination, it was proven that his stores and business model were consistently successful and that his future business prospects were strong. The combination of personal desire and business preparedness made his business an excellent candidate for franchising and he is experiencing tremendous success with his new franchise.

27

In either case detailed above, once a new franchise is developed, the owner will typically become, or continue to be intimately involved, with at least one location. Even after the franchise is developed, they will want to continually monitor how the operational and managerial systems function, and observe how Franchisee prospects and customers are responding to it. For a restaurant, they might continue to be active in menu and recipe development. In a retail operation, they might find it important to personally monitor all point-of-sale, merchandising and product selection factors, and in a service organization, monitoring quality control and maintaining positive relationships with your key customers might be top on their executive management objectives.

Further, as the Franchisor and originator of a particular business concept, you need to be involved in the growth and forward development of your organization to ensure that the franchise maintains itself as a competitively desirable business, and true to your initial concept. Aside from specific "originator" responsibilities, you will focus largely on deriving value from your trademark, managing the marketing aspects of the business, such as recruiting new Franchisees and growing market share, helping existing Franchisees get up and running, developing new markets, and building a world-class service organization your Franchisees can depend on. But, by this time, you should no longer be referring to yourself as a business owner of a Pizzeria or a Wireless Store; you should clearly see your role as a Franchisor.

note The desire to expand your business and conquer new managerial challenges is vital to your being a successful Franchisor.

With the objectives of the Franchisor becoming your major role, let us take a look further down the development timeline as you develop your franchise and explore what other issues you will face. Almost immediately, as you make the transition from business owner to Franchisor, it will become very evident to you that the legislative and regulatory climate is much more intense than anything you have likely experienced as a private business owner. Further, once you have managed to lead yourself through the seemingly painstaking regulatory disclosure and filing process, and are successful at selling your first franchise, it won't end there.

The full disclosure requirements that are set forth for preparing the Uniform Franchise Offering Circular (UFOC) and the Franchise Agreement are sadly just the beginning. The regulatory climate of the franchise industry is becoming more and more intense, not necessarily because of the industry becoming more complex, but regrettably, as this industry grows

28

and gets more and more attention, it is increasingly becoming a source for fraudulent activity. Unfortunately, there are more and more fraudulent opportunists, ill-intended service providers and prematurely developed Franchisors making it harder and harder for legitimate Franchisors to do business in this industry. To heed this, the governmental regulatory agencies have increasingly imposed additional obligations on the franchise industry, and while none of these requirements are insurmountable, they most certainly increase the time and money required to comply for a new or existing franchises.

Furthermore, most of these imposed requirements fall square under the responsibility of the franchise owner(s) or the executive management team, taking away from their availability to contribute to the direct growth of the business. You should expect that you will be spending a great deal of time initially, and a notable amount going forward, meeting with franchise developers, consultants, accountants, attorneys and other professional service providers in order to comply.

time to fill up your hat rack

In addition to the regulatory requirements, you can expect that you will be regularly needed to provide the franchise with a visible and consistent source of confidence, and at times, needed to keep the peace. During the initial growth phase of your franchise, until the unit sales become extensive enough to allow you to afford a team of professionals to help you manage the network, you will remain the person that the Franchisees look to for settling disputes, implementing requested changes for the network, granting exceptions to policy and rendering a verdict on essentially every unforeseen decision. This can prove to be time-consuming, demanding and frustrating to the new Franchisor.

Despite this, it is difficult for a new Franchisor to avoid being looked heavily upon as the main decision maker, even as you begin to bring other management into your organization, and formally develop your franchise support system. The tendency for this is strong, primarily in the first stage of growth as Franchisors develop strong relationships with "early adopters" in their franchise network.

Later, these early adopters are rarely willing to make the transition from the dependence on the founding Franchisor to the formal support team a graceful one, and generally speaking, early adopters will always look to the founder for on-going guidance concerning any operational challenge, grievance, personal request or other non-routine need.

beware Like with any new business, it is vital that the new Franchisor be excited and willing to act in many capacities while a new franchise system is developing.

30

While this roll varies from franchise to franchise, suffice it to say you will find yourself at times having to be a mediator, an accountant, a lawyer, an operations officer, a quality control officer, a job safety officer and more during the early days of your franchise. The important note here is that while this can feel and appear to be excessive "hat wearing", the experience and insight you will gain while initially responding to these needs will pay excessive dividends in your understanding first-hand how your franchise operates.

In the end, while owning a successfully developed franchise, you will find yourself being challenged and rewarded, in ways that are rarely possible as a single business owner.

CHAPTER 4

Introduction to the Franchise Development Process

My intention here is not to fully dissect the formal steps required for the development of a franchise, but to give you a sample of the requirements, steps and commitments that you will be subject to during the process. Remember, the purpose of this book is not to serve as a "how to", as it is my belief that completing the development process without even limited professional help, or with the use of a "self-help" or "software" product, is unwise. This chapter is intended only to demystify the process and provide you with an executive level summary. Please review and act accordingly.

what will it cost?

Aside from the costs for utilizing professionals service providers, the total financial investment and steps required to properly launch and fund a new franchise model can vary considerably from industry to industry. This makes it extremely difficult for me to quote you a specific cost estimate. Typically, the amount of investment that is required to adequately fund a launch will be in close ratio to the differences that you would find in funding the original business when compared to other businesses.

My point being, is that it is more affordable to fund an original business that is service based, requires little capital investment or equipment, is operated in a minimal space requirement and with limited staff than say a 400-seat restaurant that requires substantial real estate, equipment, furnishing and personnel to establish and operate. While some of the steps and costs that are incurred to start a franchise based on a large business are the same as those to start a franchise based on a small, more limited size business, many of the additional costs will be based on the complexity of the original business.

For that reason, it is important to obtain a clear

understanding of the costs that are expected for developing your specific business into a proper franchise model. This can generally be accomplished by seeking professional development services or using the guidance of an experienced franchise attorney with a strong business background that can also guide you through the business portions of the development process.

step 1: analysis of your trademark

Because a franchise is in essence simply a method of business expansion, and that the value lies heavily in the transfer and right to use an established trademark, the first step in preparing your business for franchise model distribution is to be certain that all your needed trademarks are obtained and secured.

Now, while most businesses that consider franchising have been in business for some time, and because the fundamentals of trademark law are intended to offer protection for businesses who can prove first use of a trademark, most Franchisors find little difficultly in obtaining a federal trademark. However, for others it is often at the time of franchising that they first become aware that there are one or more businesses that are currently using their exact or similar trade name, and in many cases, have already filed and obtained US Patent and Trademark protection for those trade names or marks.

Because of this possibility, the first step in the franchise development process is to research and determine if all, or any of your business' commonly used trade names, logos, word marks, service marks and other branding identifiers are available for trademark protection, or if they have already been reserved by another business prior to the date of your first using any, and all of those names or marks in trade.

34

This process involves completing a formal trademark search, both at the state and federal level to determine if any prior companies have used, or filed for protection for the use of any of your specific or similar trade names or marks. This is accomplished either by you, your franchise consultant, attorney or a professional trademark search firm, which will complete a thorough search process to determine exactly what standing your trademark or similar trademark(s) currently maintain in the market.

tip   While the Internet has made the task of Trademark Searches quicker and more accurate, the investment in a professional Trademark Search Firm is always recommended.

If the initial trademark searches reveal that another business(es) is using or has previously used one or more of your desired names or marks, or has formally filed with the US Patent and Trademark Office and obtained trademark protection, then the first obstacle your prospective franchise must overcome is deciding how to then adequately obtain protection for its market names before completing the franchise development process. Should you determine that your company trade names or marks are being used elsewhere, then you have only a few options available to you to attempt to secure the protection required for your franchise.

First, you can research further and determine whether or not the previous business(es) that have used your affected names or marks is still currently using them in commerce, or if perhaps they have discontinued the use of the marks, or have closed their business. If this is the case, there is a regulatory time period that a business can temporarily or permanently discontinue the use of its marks in the marketplace, but still maintain its exclusive rights to their use and protection thereof. If it is determined that prior use business(es) have exceeded the maximum regulatory non-use period permitted, then it is possible for your company to submit a formal filing to the US Patent and Trademark Office and seek to obtain trademark protection for those marks.

If, on the other hand, the prior use business(es) are still currently using any or all of these terms, or have not exceeded the maximum allowed non-use period, then the only way to obtain certain exclusive rights to use of the specific mark(s) is to seek out the transfer or purchase of these trademarks from the awarded business(es) either by a simple request or by a formal purchase of the rights.

Often, businesses will file trademark protection for numerous trade names and marks and never, or limitedly, use them in actual commerce. Particularly larger organizations, with access to readily available legal staff, often choose to file trademark protection on marks early in their planning stages, only to later then decide on alternative terms, slogans and names for final use in their business trade. For this reason, it is recommended that if your business' trade names or marks are previously used by another business(es), then oftentimes, you can obtain a formal ownership of these marks simply by contacting the current mark owner, explaining your business condition and requesting a transfer, either as a professional courtesy or for profit. Many businesses, if they are not using the requested mark, will be more than happy to grant or sell the marks to you and avoid further legal filing and maintenance requirements for marks they have no intention on using in the future.

In the worst-case scenario, you will find that the trade name, logo or other word identifiers that you have been using in your business for years is legally owned and protected for exclusive use by another business. Many business owners do not realize that trademark infringement is a common and largely unintended violation in our national marketplace. The fact is, when most entrepreneurs set out to start their local private businesses and select trade names and logos initially, they are largely uncertain of their company's chances for success. Most often, when our clients are informed of trademark conflicts, they respond similarly and state that they never really thought about the uniqueness and exclusivity of their trade names because at the time, they were simply trying to start a small business and never considered the future impact on their business, aside from trying to create a unique brand in their local markets.

For that reason, it is likely that most entrepreneurs reading this book will nod in agreement with the notion that when they initially set out to start their business, many of these details were looked upon only briefly as there was a sense of trial and error driving many of their business' initial decisions. In the end, it is a very common circumstance that we find older, successful businesses looking to franchise and only then realizing that they have little or no exclusive rights to their long-used trade names and/or marks.

37

beware Don't allow yourself to be "talked into" proceeding with anything but a Registered Trademark for your new Franchise. Compromising this vital step before Franchising can be fatal to a franchise.

Because franchising involves the extensive distribution nationally of a business and its brand, it is critical to obtain clear and formal trademark protection before selling a Franchisee a business and a brand that may later be challenged by a previous use business, or a business that has formally obtained a similar trademark protection. As a new Franchisor, you do not want to be faced with the complications and liability that could be imposed upon your franchise due to a trademark infringement issue.

In commerce, trademarks, on one hand can appear to be a quiet, almost unenforced concept. Each of us has encountered numerous multiple uses of names in the national business community. One simply has to travel a bit to notice the frequency of names in commerce, and acknowledge that in most cases, these conflicts can go unchallenged, as most business owners are focused solely on their local markets for abuses.

On the other hand, you will occasionally encounter news of a trademark dispute so significant, its story makes endless headline appearances and becomes a significant corporate issue. These trademark cases end far more damagingly for the accused business trademark violator, with the business being forced to modify and/or discontinue the use of a particular trade name, often with no favorable options, but to essentially re-brand their entire business from scratch, hoping that they are able to transfer as much brand goodwill as possible to the new name or logo in the consumers' eye.

So, where does this leave the new Franchisor? If you are able to obtain and protect your trade names, logos and marks with certainty, or if you have already obtained trademark protection for the marks used in your business, then this process is largely complete and you can move on to the next step in the franchise development process.

If, on the other hand, you determine that another business (es), is using or has used, or obtained protection for your business marks, and you are unsuccessful in obtaining an ownership transfer by any means, then the only alternative you have is to seek the use of a new, alternate business trademark, complete the proper searches on the newly considered marks, and if successful, file for the appropriate trademark protection.

Now, while the thought of re-naming, re-branding and re-marketing your business trade names may appear to be an insurmountable task, I can assure you that a franchise or traditional marketing firm with experience in the brand conversion process can effectively and successfully achieve this prior to your completing the franchise development process, thereby allowing you to move forward with all the appropriate trademark protection and first-class branding needed to launch a successful franchise.

So, trademark issues alone should not dissuade you from entering franchising. The emphasis here is intended to urge preparation and clarification to avoid damaging surprises later, not to discourage you from allowing your business to benefit from the power of franchising.

Again, because the essence of franchising relies so heavily on the ability to share use of a strong brand's identity and trademark, it is essentially impossible to recommend that a business owner with questionable trademark protection go forward with a franchise development plan.

step 2: the feasibility test

Once you have made the determination that franchising your business is the ideal expansion method for your business, it is important before you do anything else, to complete an extensive feasibility study on your business and the industry that it operates within.

Feasibility studies give the Franchisor an accurate and honest insight into his or her business' chances of success and, if executed properly and completely, will reveal most opportunities, threats and market factors that will affect the developed franchise's future. For those of you not familiar with the term feasibility study, let me describe what is involved.

The feasibility study is essentially the exploration of the market factors and business issues that do, or can affect your business, and ultimately, your franchise. A proper feasibility study will include an extensive competitive analysis of all current and potentially emerging competitive businesses, a review and analysis of your current business' condition, and what issues has effected or can effect its success, the observation of any current or pending regulatory or licensure requirements for doing business in your industry, how changes in the regulatory environment can impact your franchise, analysis of current and expected consumer demand trends, and an impact study on any of the current or impending factors that you can identify as critical to the future success of your business and your franchise.

beware Don't assume that you are fully aware of vital business and industry factors. More often than not, a Feasibility Study will uncover material issue(s) unfamiliar to a business owner.

By completing a study of this nature, it is the first in a series of steps that not only will competently prepare you to develop the strategy and the system that you will use to franchise your business, but it also allows you and your consultants the opportunity to identify issues that are of concern, and execute any needed action plans to correct them, as well as validating any assumptions that are made during the franchise development process about your business, your franchise, the market, or your industry specifically.

At the conclusion of an effective feasibility study, providing that your franchise is one that merits full development, you should derive a strong sense of confidence and encouragement about the future of your business and your franchise. If, on the other hand, the conclusions made following your feasibility study raise concern for the appropriateness and likelihood of success for your franchise, then it is important to take a pause and identify those issues that are in your control and can be corrected, or recognize there may be factors beyond the business' control that threaten the success of the franchise model.

The key to achieving beneficial results from a feasibility study is honesty. When I personally interview potential Franchisors while completing the feasibility study exercise, it is important for me to be aware when they are responding to a question that causes them concern.

Many times, a business owner will openly or instinctually know that his or her business is being negatively affected by a particular issue or threat, but when considering how that same issue or threat will impact a future Franchisee location, will assert the belief that the same issue will not have an impact on any of the Franchisees.

41

So, as you review the appropriateness of your business as an extended franchise model, ask yourself honestly, what issues currently affect your business and what issues you fear will affect your business in the future, and be forthcoming enough to admit that without their resolution or adaptation, then it is likely that any developed franchise network will face the same. While franchise networks clearly benefit from your personal experience and your business' success, it is equally important to leverage your knowledge, and willfully acknowledge that your Franchisees will almost always be faced with the same pre-franchise development problems as well.

step 3: preparation of the required regulatory documents

Once you have completed a thorough feasibility study and

made the determination that franchising remains the expansion method of choice for your business, the first step in the formal franchise development process is the drafting of the required regulatory and legal documents required for the legal sale of a franchise. These consist primarily of the UFOC, or Uniform Franchise Offering Circular and the accompanying Franchise Agreement. The commonly referred to UFOC is the Holy Grail of the franchise regulatory environment.

Franchising has evolved rapidly over the last thirty years, having largely grown from a private one-on-one transaction based industry, to one that is challenged by ever-increasing federal and state regulatory requirements. This trend began in 1978, when the Federal Trade Commission officially required the UFOC from all Franchisors, and it continues to be refined, with the ultimate goal of offering better protection to the consumer and increasing the disclosure and accurate representation of a franchise offering. The continued changes that have been imposed on the regulatory landscape have largely been due to the continued fraudulent activity of would-be Franchisors preying on ill-informed consumers, selling what in many cases amounted to franchise format businesses with little or no ability to achieve profits.

Now, while honest Franchisors are the victims of what has evolved into more expensive and more time-consuming regulatory requirements, it is clear that completing the exercise of full disclosure helps even the most honest Franchisor determine whether his or her franchise truly meets the criteria needed to effectively offer a quality franchise, and provides some assurances that the buying Franchisee stands a reasonable chance of earning the anticipated return on their investment.

So what exactly is the UFOC? The UFOC is largely a disclosure document. Its sections, paragraphs, and contents are strictly asserted in the preparation instructions issued by the

Federal Trade Commission (FTC). This means that the content in the document should minimally meet specific disclosure objectives and must include specific requested information as ordered by the Federal Trade Commission.

beware The UFOC, while commonly considered by many business owners and industry professionals as a "template", requires thorough, custom legal preparation to be effective.

So, while the Franchisor can exceed the minimum disclosure requirements and move to further disclose his or her franchise offering, it is expected that each Franchisor prepares and legally certifies with a bar admitted attorney, that he or she has properly completed the fiduciary task of preparing the disclosure document. Once completed, the UFOC should provide a prospective Franchisee, with little or no previous knowledge of the franchise, with an accurate and complete review of the specific terms, conditions, requirements, and costs that will be imposed on him or her if a franchise purchase is made.

The preparation of a UFOC is completed in essentially two steps. The first step is personal and verbal in nature. You will need a competent franchise consultant or franchise attorney that will not only spend the time necessary to meet with you and your management team, tour your facilities and review your operations adequately enough to determine not only what information and requirements of the UFOC are evident, but also help you specifically structure the franchise offering. It is critical to spend the adequate amount of time to analyze your current business processes and operations, evaluate your financial history, review and/or establish trademark protection, complete feasibility studies, evaluate your competition, and much more, before beginning the

UFOC drafting process.

The list below is a representation of what business and legal areas should be analyzed while preparing the UFOC and structuring the franchise system, with a brief description of the content present in each section.

Be sure to review the UFOC specimen in Appendix A for a specific example of how these analysis areas are presented in a working document.

Franchisee / Franchisor Obligations

Put simply, this section is an itemization of the compulsory responsibilities that will be required of both the Franchisee and the Franchisor throughout the term of the Franchise Agreement.

44

Franchisee Investment Requirements

Details the investment requirements, dollar amounts, payment recipients and time due for the investments needed to develop a legally compliant and operational franchise system.

Earnings Estimates

If provided, an Earning Estimate provides franchise prospects with a disclosure of the revenue and income expected to operate a typical franchise location described for sale. Although the trend is changing, at this time the majority of Franchisors avoid preparing and disclosing Earnings in their UFOC's. This is in part due to the expense, and the legal liability sometimes associated with making the earnings commitments to buyers, should the units not produce as estimated.

Financial Statement Analysis

Although not formally disclosed in the UFOC, a detailed analysis of a business' current financial statement is recommended before any formal franchise development decisions are made. It is critical to identify any revenue opportunities that may be present in the current business, but cannot be duplicated at the franchise level. Similarly, if there are financial risks not present at the concept business, but are expected to be encountered at the franchise outlets, then these impacts need to be analyzed appropriately.

Business Entity Determination

Before any franchise offering, it is important to form a new business entity to shield your existing business and personal assets from any liabilities or claims that may emerge from franchise related claims in the future. Because there are many corporate formation options, it is important to analyze which method is best for you and your business based on your specific criteria.

45

Royalties and Franchisee Fees

Perhaps the most elaborate analysis, determining the proper on-going royalties and fees and the initial franchise fee payable is critical to your franchise's growth, future profitability, competitive preparedness and Franchisee satisfaction. More than any other area, this analysis requires an intelligent mix of quantitative and qualitative analysis, and a fair amount of business experience and instinct to complete properly.

Marketing/Trademark Usage & Guidelines

Because the assignment of use of a business' trademark(s) and other intellectual property is at the essence of franchising's definition, it is critical to determine who, where, how and for how long, a Franchisee is granted the rights for use of these assets. Even more important is determining whether a business has obtained proper trademark and/or patent rights from the appropriate governmental bodies, and is truly legally qualified to transfer such rights in the first place, and/or whether any formal filings are still required by the Franchisor.

Handling Franchisee Disputes

Disputes in franchising are inevitable. The nature of franchising requires significant monetary and time investment from individuals who, quite frankly, despite any amount of disclosure, expect success. For this reason, and countless others, when Franchisee expectations are not met, Franchisors generally bear the brunt of the blame.

46

As with any worthwhile venture, some challenges are expected, and an adequate analysis of the best course of action for handling disputes can make your franchising experience considerably less stressful, and protect your franchise system from time consuming and costly disputes that can injure the system's participant morale.

Agreement Term & Renewal Factors

Depending on such factors as total investment required, build-out and build-up time, product demand trends, market maturity, franchise fee determination, intellectual property rights and other factors, the Agreement and Renewal terms of your contract will vary. A close examination of these factors will lead to a safe determination of the correct contract terms needed.

Terminating Problem Franchisees

Handling Franchisee disputes and designing a resolution system to increase the likelihood of a mutually satisfying settlement is necessary to avoid most Franchisee terminations. However, Franchisee terminations are a part of the franchise ownership process. In order to reduce or eliminate legal complications following any termination, it is necessary to establish a clear and communicated dispute and termination process that is disclosed before and throughout the termination process.

When developing a franchise, you will determine what factors should necessitate a termination, and disclose all related steps and remedies available to both parties during the process.

Technology and the Franchisor

47

I personally think technology is a main ingredient to the recent success and growth of franchising in America and abroad. Technology enables Franchisors to provide more services, information and support to their franchise systems in less time, and with considerably less investment per unit. Similarly, technology aids each Franchisee in marketing their local units and helping each spend more time working "in" the businesses rather the "on" their business. Additionally, technology is essential in maintaining a consistent system-wide brand across all advertising mediums now available to the franchise industry (ie. Internet, print, television, radio, in-store marketing, etc.).

For this, it is an important step to determine a definitive technology policy and procedures for a franchise, and be certain that the critical elements of the policy is reflected in the legally binding agreement(s) to ensure compliance.

Books & Record Keeping

While franchising at its roots is a highly trusting business structure, with seeming strangers making significant investments into organizations that they have very limited personal familiarization with, there is of course cause for concern, and the need for prevention of financial misgivings.

tip The UFOC, while required, allows you to take a detailed review of your business that is rarely performed without necessity, and the results often pay high dividends to the prototype business.

Like all business relationships, there will be a minority of Franchisees that either initially, or further down the relationship tenure, seek to take advantage of the system and commit varying levels of unethical financial maneuvering. For this reason, a properly analyzed and designed financial reporting system for your franchise, with specific requirements, obligations and consequences for abuse should be developed and enforced.

48

Franchise Sales & Transfer Conditions

While essentially all of your initial Franchisee engagements will involve a lot of talk about permanent and long-lasting relationships, things change, and Franchisees need to have options to sell and transfer ownership in their franchise unit(s). For this, a plan designed to give the Franchisor first rights of refusal to purchase units for sale is the general rule, however, analyzing you and your business' requirements and goals is important to determine the best course of action regarding compulsory sale and transfer conditions for existing franchise units.

my ufoc summary

At this point, I want to take a step back and reassure you that while many franchise lawyers and franchise developers focus heavily and emotionally on the preparation of UFOC, mostly in an effort to demand high compensation for their services, that the UFOC is largely a boilerplate, tested and structured document.

For this reason, although it is recommended that you seek the professional services of either an appropriately resourced franchise development firm or an experienced franchise attorney, it is recommended more for the analysis and the proper structuring of your franchise rather than the necessity of the physical preparation of UFOC. There are far too many franchise developers and franchise attorneys in our industry that impose fear in the hearts of a would-be Franchisor based on the impact of the UFOC and the Franchise Agreement. In fact, I myself once made anonymous calls to many of the leading industry service providers and I was shocked to find the number that focus strictly and limitedly on the preparation of the UFOC as the main emphasis for their existence, and your payment.

In my opinion, you would be far better served seeking such professional assistance for the structuring of your franchise and understanding that the majority of the content that is included in the UFOC is mandated by the Federal Trade Commission, and not included based on the infinite wisdom of a high-priced franchise consultant or franchise attorney.

Now, this assertion is not the first time I have made this opinion public. I regularly tell not only my prospects of our business, but the press and other industry insiders that I am concerned and embarrassed at times to be involved in this industry when so many of our proclaimed professionals are seemingly ripping off their clients by delivering a couple of legal documents and neglecting so much more of the franchise development process.

So, while I tread lightly not to minimize the importance or the significance of UFOC, as it is a critical document to the establishment and protection of the parties' rights that agree to it, I am simply stating for the record that it is only a part of what is minimally required to launch a successful franchise organization. Do not believe anyone in our industry that tells you that the legal documents are the majority of the basis of your franchise development requirements. These legal documents simply allow you the legal opportunity to sell your franchise. It is the equivalent of obtaining a driver's license for an automobile; it only allows you the privilege to participate, but in no way assures you a quality, safe experience.

step 4: drafting the franchise operations manual

The next step in the franchise development process is the drafting and assembly of a comprehensive Franchise Operations Manual. At the heart of any franchise is the system. In fact, on close examination, what a Franchisee is really buying is a system. Although this system will be accompanied by a history of branding, goodwill, name recognition and quality product(s), it is the execution of the franchise system that makes a Franchisee successful.

To illustrate the importance of an adequate and professionally prepared franchise operations manual, let me illustrate a typical Franchisee buyer analysis exercise. Whenever a prospective Franchisee looks to your business as a potential investment opportunity, he is really asking himself one question. Should I buy or build my business?

What this means is that at the root of every franchise transaction is the analysis of whether or not a buyer would be more rewarded by buying an existing business model or building an original business from scratch. In fact, if you were to take yourself back to the moment that you started your current business, assuming that this business was started by you, and not bought or inherited from another individual, it is likely that you did, or would have experienced the same sense of choice.

A good franchise offering provides a random Franchisee with a higher rate of success, an accelerated breakeven point and with a more rapid and greater level of profitability. If a franchise did not offer a franchise buyer the opportunity to start a business more rapidly and gain a return on his investment at an accelerated rate, it is unlikely it would gain any growth momentum at all.

If the franchise industry and the offerings in it merely put the franchise buyer at an even keel to the risks, costs and likely returns to his developing his own unique original business, then except for those who have no business skill set at all, it is highly probable that buyers would simply invest in themselves. The Franchise Operations Manual and the system described and presented in it is a significant part of the franchise offering and provides the franchise buyer the means to meet the objective of achieving a more rapid return on investment, and a higher probability for success.

51

tip A well-drafted Franchise Operation Manual represents a material source of confidence for a franchise buyer and the final publication(s) should be reflective of their investment.

Additionally, without taking the time to provide a thorough knowledge transfer from the Franchisor to the Franchisee, what is it that you are really selling? For this reason, it is critical for a new Franchisor to take the necessary time, and dedicate the professional resources needed to properly prepare and present a quality Franchise Operations Manual.

So, what should be included? Answering this question is simple. An operations manual should include all the required information, resources and tools for a brand new Franchisee, who never encountered any hands-on experience with your business, to open, grow and operate your business independently.

This means, at the very minimum, the Franchise Operations Manual for your franchise should cover the operational tasks of running your business extensively. For every business, this will vary, as there are some businesses that require an enormous amount of intellectual information to prepare a new Franchisee to operate the business.

For instance, my firm has a franchise client that is a pool construction company. So, aside from having to detail all the operational steps required to sell, permit, bill, service and manage the company's pool projects and its clients, it was also necessary to prepare and author numerous volumes of information to instruct new pool construction Franchisees on the exacting process of physically building a pool.

So, as you can imagine, there was an enormous required knowledge transfer that this Franchisor's Operations Manual had to accomplish. The lesson here is not to specifically detail all the contents that you should consider including in your Franchise Operations Manual. It is simply to make you aware that this step is an important and vital one to developing a franchise business model that can achieve your success with minimal personal involvement by your staff, and gives your new Franchisee a fair chance to replicate the exacting qualities that made your business so successful to date.

Be certain, whether you prepare these manuals yourself,

with the help of your staff or using the services of an outside development team, that your Franchise Operations Manual covers more, much more, then basic information. And, that it dives deeply into the specifics that make your company unique.

One last thought on this subject: if you are successful at preparing these documents in a complete and comprehensive way, what you will have accomplished would allow any individual the means to review the Franchise Operations Manual materials and essentially replicate your business. For a franchise buyer, this is the minimum expectation. However, in the hands of a competitor or an individual that has not compensated you appropriately, these manuals can be used destructively against your company. Once your franchise begins to grow, be certain that you and your staff are doing everything possible to maintain the confidentiality of these manuals. It is important to include a detailed confidentiality agreement, and have each franchise execute this agreement, before granting him or her a set of these manuals.

Equally important is to regain possession of the manuals each time a Franchisee is terminated, closes his business, transfers ownership to another party or retires. Further, I would urge any Franchisor who feels that a party has compromised the security of the manuals to either revoke his possession of them or seek a legal remedy to regain them should they fall into the hands of a third party due to a Franchisee's neglect.

53

CHAPTER 5

Branding & Marketing for Franchisors

a marketing fairy tale

In franchising, as in business, marketing is everything. When I speak with clients and prospects, I choose to talk about marketing and branding from a visual and perceptual standpoint. We discuss the emotions, feelings, satisfactions and confidences that a good brand has on their business's valuation, and their opinions of the companies that they have been exposed to. Now, in that spirit, I'd like to as closely as possible present that verbal exercise and discuss a current marketing and branding scenario present in our marketplace. To illustrate the importance and impact of quality branding and marketing on a business, consider the following.

Let us use Apple Computers for our example. (Note: I am an Apple user, but reluctantly typing this book using a Microsoft Windows book writing application) If you have been watching this company and its recent growth, then their clean, modern and stylish design elements and excellent use of imagery in their branding have surely caught your attention. Apple has successfully transformed their Apple icon into not only a universally recognized, but also highly admired brand element.

In fact, when preparing my notes for this book, and questioning associates about their opinion of the company, I heard on a surprising number of occasions that the Apple logo and brand actually makes its customers "feel good". What Apple has managed to do is embed their "feel good" products, such as the Apple iPod music player, with their brand. It was described that some of them experience elicited emotions simply from seeing the logo or branding images similar to those that they experience while listening to their favorite music on the company's best-selling music player.

Similarly, if you ask most Apple customers what they think of Apple, you will be shocked at the emotion and energy that many express in their responses. So it seems, again at the hand of an original company founder, Apple has quickly transformed itself from a customer base of cult following Anti-Microsoft critics, to a brand where essentially all demographic segments of the buying public have begun the process of becoming "Apple Fanatics".

Now, I know I am biased. I have already mentioned that I am a fan of Apple and the products they produce. But, what I have witnessed from this company in the past four years has been, in my opinion, among the best concert of branding, marketing and product development that I have ever seen.

Apple successfully executed an award-winning marketing and branding campaign, while managing to produce award-winning products at the same time. And, while I don't believe that their newfound success is based solely on their products, similarly, the company would not have achieved even a fraction of the success they are experiencing without superb marketing.

56

Looking back, Apple customers and critics alike have always characterized the company as having excellent products. Apple recently broke through by executing a top-of-mind marketing campaign AND emerging with a product line, that in short order, has become a common sight in essentially every public place: the iPod.

To experience Apple's marketing savvy for yourself, start by spending some time on Apple's Website, then visit one of their retail stores, and finally buy one, any one, of their products. Your experience from your first moment of brand exposure, to the opening and inspecting of the simplest packaging design and contents, will give you an intense marketing and branding experience that is among the best I have studied. Every moment of an Apple customer's experience, down to the smallest detail, is analyzed and intended to continually reinforce the Apple experience.

This level of intentional marketing and branding should be the goal of any business wishing to grow and leave a lasting impression on their customers, and is a vital requirement for the success of any franchise. Without it, a franchise organization is likely to fail, remain vulnerable to competition or experience only temporary success.

take the franchise branding and marketing test

Now, I know what you are thinking. Apple is a huge company and has essentially limitless resources available to it and its marketing efforts. Admittedly, I would agree, a company with the financial size and capabilities of Apple would certainly appear to have a daunting advantage over a start up in their industry. Any new would-be computer manufacturer would have a significant challenge presenting its products to the marketplace with the intention and frequency that Apple can, and if you were to call me and say you would like to become the next Dell or Apple Computer, I would probably wish you luck knowing full well that I knew your chances for success were miniscule.

In franchising, however, there are numerous marketing expansion options available to the Franchisor to control expansion both geographically and financially, and provide the Franchisor with growth options that a company that sets out to rule the computer industry simply does not have.

By now, you have established your business model and closely perfected the operational issues in your business, or franchising would not be an available expansion option for you in the first place.

If you were to simply meet the minimal regulatory requirements and immediately start franchising with an amateur or inadequate marketing strategy and branding, it is likely you will encounter one of two outcomes. One: that the franchise will suffer a slow and painful growth rate, with your initial Franchisee's accusatory and frustrated with your offered marketing resources, and their demanding an enterprise class marketing solution to regain or remain competitive.

beware Remember, a franchise business just another business to consumers. They don't care about UFOC's, regulations or system structure. They demand superb marketing to get their attention.

Or two: you could fail to grow substantially at all, and revert back to your initial business, frustrated and confused over the reasons why former Franchisees were not successful with the results of your franchise's marketing plan, when executed in their new franchise territories, where your business was unfamiliar.

58

Without naming prospects, I will cautiously admit that although I daily meet gifted and capable business owners who talk to me about franchising, the large majority of them either do not understand the importance of marketing in their business, or simply disregard the need altogether. Many of them have had their original businesses grow organically in their local markets and they confidently project this success as something that would be easily replicated by all their future Franchisees.

Most fail to put honest credit where due, and conveniently forget about the fact that their successful restaurant is located in a neighborhood where three generations of their family have lived, or that their health club is the only one within twenty miles of its location. Furthermore, most clients grossly overestimate their particular business's ability to thrive in a new state, or even a few miles away, where their business is largely unknown and will simply blend into the fabric of a consumer's many choices.

Furthermore, when I attempt to emphasize the importance of marketing and branding, most owners reply with "my marketing is fine and I don't want to change a thing", and later share that their logo was created by a nephew or the like who is a "good artist", and/or that their Website was programmed by their son or daughter who "is great on a computer". This insistence on what I call "staying small", is where I regularly first encounter a challenge in having my new Franchisor clients let go of the "owner" aspect of his business and begin to adapt to the "Franchisor" role.

beware   "Local" business success does not mean "National" success. It is critically important to determine if your business can compete nationally before franchising.

59

Marketing and branding development is the one area of the franchise development process that I insist that my clients "let go" of, and allow the business to be analyzed from a professional, and not a personal perspective. The fact is, it is highly neglectful attempting to build what you hope will be a national brand on a nephew's logo or a child's work. It not only puts the franchise at risk from the inception, but also, in my opinion, neglects one of the fiduciary duties that a Franchisor has to its Franchisees before taking their money.

So, as you look forward to the possibility of franchising your business, ask yourself; does my company set itself apart from the competition? Is my logo and identity world-class, with a distinct and memorable uniqueness? Does my store or business environment reinforce my company's public identity? Do my marketing communication pieces accurately reflect my business's true product offerings? Is my marketing and design professional enough to visualize being used on a national scale? Do my current customers comment favorably on my existing marketing and design elements? And, an important question; Do I envy or admire a competitor's marketing, advertising or identity, or do I think of any of them as superior?

When you ask these most important questions and allow for personal and honest reflection, then despite whether you have had any professional marketing experience or education, it will become vividly clear where your business measures on this important issue.

If upon reflection, you concur with the need for change and improvement, then by all means, let personal history and relations stand aside and invest in a professional marketing and identity makeover BEFORE setting out to formally franchise your business. I can all but promise you that for every dollar you invest on quality marketing efforts, your business will produce exponential returns in both franchise unit and system-wide product sales in the future.

60

Remember, it is likely that a large majority of your franchise units will be located in areas that have never heard of your business before, and in order for these units to succeed, they will be required to compete with other locally, well established and national brands. Not providing the very best marketing and branding resources to the new Franchisee will almost certainly risk either their unit's failure or at best, their utter dissatisfaction with your abilities, both of which are disastrous.

Finally, remember that when you emerge from the franchise development process and initially begin to sell your franchises, you will likely be competing head-to-head against established Franchisors in your industry. That said, it is critical that your franchise's marketing and branding be the best it will be for the entire history of your franchise, on the first day of its launch, not the last. I regularly assert to my new clients and prospects that Subway Sandwiches could sell their franchises from a napkin, now that their franchise, and its reputation is fully developed.

All too often, because of a combination of bad advice, monetary urgency, or their franchise developer's lack of ability or human resources, Franchisors race to "start selling" in a state of lack of preparedness, which often temporarily or permanently stalls the system's growth, until the owners come to the realization that marketing is critical, and make the investments and dedicate the time to develop an enviable marketing program, designed for success.

analyzing your business' marketing strategy

Because marketing is an ongoing process, a business owner must continually measure and analyze the demand for the company's products and services. Completing a marketing analysis is an effective way of determining the current state of your business and whether there is much to be done before franchising.

note Most Franchisors once operated businesses with no formal planning process. As a rule, local success remains isolated and a Marketing Strategy must be established to grow beyond your original market(s).

In addition to determining the level of consumer demand for a company's products and services, a Franchisor must also analyze its current strengths and weaknesses, how it markets its products and services, whether it can more effectively do so, and what it can and cannot do to initiate changes in consumer demand.

Further, a responsible Franchisor should regularly monitor industry trends, political and social changes, environmental and legal issues, and technology and competitive offerings in order to be certain that the company's products and services maintain their competitive characteristics and advantages.

To start, an effective analysis technique for reviewing the quality of a marketing program is called the "Four P's", and represents the product, place, price and promotion of a franchise marketing plan. This strategy recognizes the importance of these components, and when analyzed, allows the Franchisor to create the ideal marketing mix for its products and services.

tip   The Four P's – Product, Place, Price and Promotion are excellent marketing components to examine when developing a formal marketing plan.

62

"Product" refers to which products and services the Franchisor will offer to its consumers. By analyzing your products, you can determine whether the products and services offered will differ based on whether they are delivered through a Franchisee location or company-owned center. Additionally, features, options, styles, sizes, quality levels and other unique characteristics make up the product segment and need to be analyzed.

"Place" refers to the manner in which a Franchisor will distribute its product and services. Distribution can be channeled directly through company-owned locations, Franchisee locations and/or a hybrid of Internet mail order or other direct marketing methods. It is important to define which specific distribution methods the franchise network will be permitted to use, and whether the Franchisee or company-owned centers will have differing distribution methods available to them.

It is also important to regularly analyze the advantages and disadvantages of each of your distribution methods and determine whether preferable alternatives exist. More specifically, a Franchisor should be aware of how a specific location will affect the Franchisee's ability to market its product and services. For instance, in some geographic locations, there may be significantly stronger or measurably weaker competitive offerings, or the population of an area may simply not support one or more or the available distribution methods.

This analysis is the start of what will ultimately become the structuring of the franchise territory strategy. In order to determine what and where franchise territories will be available for sale, a Franchisor must know clearly what "place" factors are important in designing a territory assignment system that is to be successful.

63

"Price" is a measure of what a consumer is willing to pay for a franchise's product or service. Price is an important analysis step because it not only provides a key differentiator between a Franchisee's products and services and those of his competitors, but it also allows a Franchisor to determine how much local control should be given to a Franchisee for pricing determinations at the local level.

If the Franchisor determines that price sensitivities exist for his product or service, then it is likely that local Franchisees will require pricing controls to remain locally competitive. By allowing pricing flexibility, Franchisees can react quickly to remain competitively priced in each local market. On the other hand, making incorrect pricing assumptions can have a lasting impact on the franchise network. In general, professional pricing studies should be completed regularly for the entire geographic area(s) that the franchise network will operate in.

The final analysis point is "Promotion". Promotion is the determination and establishment of what strategies should be implemented to be certain that the consumer public is aware of the company's products and services. More specifically, it determines what sales, marketing, advertising and public relations plans will be used to execute the overall objectives of the franchise marketing plan. This can range from designation and assignment of services provided by outside vendors, to determining how internal resources, both human and financial, will be allocated in order to execute the promotion objectives.

Only when the above marketing and promotional analysis and discussion is completed, should the formal process of establishing a marketing strategy for the franchise begin.

CHAPTER 6
_____

Other Factors That Impact Your Chances for Success

is your franchise likable?

As a business model, franchising maintains an envious success rate, and I feel incredibly optimistic about franchising as an industry. In the United States, franchising not only allows consumers to do business with a predictable result and competitive prices, but it also allows consumers to shop the country with a similar comfort and confidence that would otherwise only be available to them in their hometowns.

On the other hand, if you look critically at franchising, as some critics and Americans do, there is an underlying opinion that franchising is creating a generic America, sometimes referred to as "Generica". The presumption is that franchising is deteriorating the "local experience" in our small towns and cities, as franchises become more dominant across the American landscape.

This is best characterized by the "sameness notion". That as you travel the United States, you will repeatedly see the "same" from coast-to-coast: the same restaurants, the same big box stores, the same lodging facilities, the same gas stations and convenience stores, and the same entertainment outlets.

Now, while that might be an accurate assessment and evidence that we may be losing some unique appeal in our local towns and neighborhoods, I believe that given the choice, people would rather do business with companies and organizations that they are comfortable with, companies they have had positive experiences with, and ones that will consistently provide the products and services they are satisfied with.

That said, it is evident to me that if you enter franchising with a business model that possesses the characteristics required to be successful, then you stand a good chance of not only being successful, but also capturing the hearts and minds of the critics who resent franchise growth, and with a product or service worthy of national consumption and demand.

is investment capital readily available?

Generally speaking, there are several economic factors that dictate the ideal maximum investment target for individual franchise buyers. Among these are competition, national economic conditions, interest rates, employment rates and inflation. The most notable in the last six to eight years (2000+), however, has been the high availability of home equity values for US homeowners.

tip Work hard to create a franchise offering that is flexible and appropriate in order to attract the largest qualified franchise prospect pool possible.

68

Franchisors marketing franchise offerings within this time period have enjoyed having an ample supply of franchise prospects with access to readily available home equity accounts having sizable value. The majority of franchise purchase funding has come from these accounts and other equity lending products.

For instance, if an individual was displaced from a long-term position or moved into retirement and explored franchising as a next step, it was typically easy for him to raise the capital to buy most franchise opportunities simply by accessing available home equity accounts. Because the majority of the amounts available were between one-hundred and two-hundred thousand dollars, it is important to recognize that measurably exceeding this amount limits a Franchisee prospect pool considerably and begins to push the "envelope of affordability".

Once you do so, then you have to consider how you will attract a Franchisee prospect pool that has been able to accumulate wealth beyond what they have been able to earn from real estate appreciation and savings. Furthermore, if your offering far exceeds these averages, then it is likely that your individual franchise buyers will either be forced to substantially risk their personal savings or retirement accounts, or be required to access third-party funding or lending as well.

Additionally, if the recent home equity resource is threatened, or availability declines, then Franchisors will be pressured to either reduce start-up costs, offering varying business models, or create financing options. Home equity extraction tends to rise in line with property values, and declines on the way down; no homeowner wants to borrow against a deflating asset, and no bank wants to secure a loan against one.

So, barring the development of another readily available investment funding source, Franchisors are urged to position their investor requirements as flexibly as possible, and pay close attention to capital availability for franchise purchasers.

69

are the regulators on your side?

Another factor that could have an impact on your chances of success is the regulatory environment in your business' industry. If your business operates in an industry that encounters a great deal of regulatory restriction, then it is possible that future regulatory changes could have a dramatic impact on the growth of your franchise network.

Now, while there are some industries that are regularly impacted by regulation, such as pest control, lending, credit repair, medical services and insurance, the majority only occasionally face sweeping regulatory change. If on review, you suspect that the regulatory environment for your industry may soon encounter change that creates a significantly more restricted business climate, then it is wise for you to avoid franchising at this time and determine conclusively, if those changes will substantially affect your industry.

is your competition manageable?

Competition is yet another material, obvious success factor. While there are generally opportunities for innovative entrepreneurs, in the most established industries, where significant players exist, it is more difficult, and considerably more expensive to make a lasting competitive stand. While there certainly are a number of success stories of franchises that have succeeded against established, big players in markets such as restaurants and foodservice, the rental industries and retail, competing head-to-head against a three-hundred-pound gorilla while expanding nationally is, understandably daunting and risky.

70

beware Never underestimate competition, or assume that your franchising efforts exclude you from the threats of current competitors. Each can respond accordingly and remain a threat to your business if not closely monitored.

If your current business is being impacted or significantly threatened by one or more largely affecting competitor(s), then it is expected the same pressures will impact your growing franchise network. It is important to analyze the competitive landscape for your industry and decide for yourself (or with professional help), whether your franchise can sustainably compete, and whether a new Franchisor will be equipped to prevail in their local markets.

is technology part of you plan?

Technology always needs to be addressed when determining the likelihood of success in franchising. Technology has created limitless opportunities for new and existing franchising businesses, and has essentially made others obsolete.

More compelling are the markets that are currently in the throes of technology revolutions that will significantly impact all or some of their business processes. These impacts can create new opportunities as well as threats, and in many industries, it is undecided how these technology trends will affect them in the future.

One example is the video industry. There are many predictions that the videotape rental market will gravely suffer directly due to technology advances. One such advance is the ability to use technology to offer a direct sales model similar to Netflix, where while working at a significantly reduced cost structure, this provider can reach essentially any market, and offer a video rental service door-to-door, at a very affordable price.

This sales, marketing and distribution model was simply not available as the retail giants, such as Blockbuster, began their market dominance. And today, providers such as Blockbuster are finding themselves reacting to competitors that just a few years ago, could not have been conceived. Further still, while Netflix flexes their marketing muscle, yet another contender, Video On-Demand (VOD), is entering the arena only because of further technological advances.

In fact, depending on what articles you read, predictions have ranged from total annihilation of traditional video rental business, to the forced sale of the traditional shops to the VOD leaders. The suppositions being that soon we will all be ordering the entertainment of our choice, at the exact time of our choice, all from the set-top box already provided by cable or a satellite television company.

Technology is changing so rapidly that traditional businesses, such as tutoring and education, courier and delivery services, and printing services that relied on face-to-face contact for their business interaction can now deliver much of their services virtually.

So, if a prospective Franchisor has managed to amass a small chain of successful, highly profitable local video rental stores, it is only prudent to honestly assess these mentioned, and other known threats, before confirming the decision to franchise. By analyzing the opportunities and the threats that technology is expected to have on your specific industry in the coming years, only then can you offer a franchise with conviction to an unsuspecting, inexperienced franchise buyer.

Threats notwithstanding, and aside from the competitive and market impacts that technology will have on your business and franchising in general, you should be aware that as a Franchisor, you will be expected to use the power of technology to serve and support your Franchisees as well. If at this time, you are not using technology in your business, it will be essential to engage professional service providers to assist you in creating and providing the technology needed to manage and support a distributed group of Franchisees.

Today, it is becoming increasingly expected that Franchisors offer Franchisees electronic, 24/7 access to all essential franchise information and resources, a localized website for their use in marketing to their local markets, any technology needed to serve their clients competitively and effectively, and the means to access marketing material at a moment's notice.

Be certain that should you decide to franchise your

business, that you select a development service provider that can provide these technologies in a proven way. Trying to stand out in a crowded market as a Franchisor with no technology value proposition to offer effectively tells the franchise buyer that you are not ready to adequately support them.

how will consolidation impact your franchise?

If your business operates in an industry or segment currently undergoing consolidation (the reduction of competitors by merger or failure) then it is logical that your customer base has or will diminish as well. One example of this involved a Franchisor prospect whose business was installing, servicing and maintaining POS (point of sale) systems, engineered specifically for multi-lane grocery stores.

73

beware Many new Franchisors see technology as an "after franchising" exercise. Make no mistake, Franchisees now demand and except exceptional franchise support and marketing technology from the onset of a new franchise system.

As a consumer yourself, I am certain you have noticed in your state, the continued consolidation of large grocery stores. In fact, in most states there are as little as two dominating players remaining.

Now, because his product was specific to such a niche market, it was imperative for him, and the Franchisees that would buy his territories, to have an ample supply of independent grocery stores to market too. Therefore, with the current market forces present, it would be exceedingly difficult for him to build a successful franchise network when the only buyers are a small number of nationalized or regional grocery stores chains that likely make purchasing decisions from a centralized office. As expected, this prospect chose another expansion method, as franchising was clearly not an ideal choice for his market conditions.

From this example, we should learn that before going forward with a franchise development model, and begin selling territories, we must carefully analyze the consolidation trends that can impact our product and service markets. Generally speaking, the less buyers you have for your product or service, the less sellers needed, and consequently, less franchise opportunity. If your industry is experiencing increasingly diminished or declining buyers market due to consolidation, expanding your business through franchising will most certainly prove counter-productive, and will most likely end in failure as the trend plays out over time.

74

will consumer tastes continue to like the flavor of your franchise?

Consumer tastes is another impact that you have to consider when contemplating franchising your business. Consumer tastes can change relatively rapidly, and while basing past success on future results is an accepted metric in business, careful attention needs to be used when dealing with product and service areas that are new, trendy or untraditional, as Americans can prove frighteningly finicky and disloyal to new ideas. One such condition to be cautious of before deciding on long-term product or service demand is the market forces caused by a fad.

There are countless examples of how business has been impacted, either by intentionally setting out to create and operate in a "fad" lifecycle, or by falling victim to a fad definition in the marketplace. Typically, a business concept can be characterized as a fad if;

1. A product (or service) catapults to high popularity and then demand all but dies off within eighteen months.

2. Cyclical demand for a product appears every six or seven years for brief periods.

3. Product demand recurs generationally, about every ten to fifteen years, or if it continues, a wave-like demand curve is developed, with extreme highs and lows.

One example is the ever frequent fad diet product cycle. Many numerous franchise organizations have developed based on diet products and services, some still with us today and many gone. One recent example of this trend is the Atkins Organization, and it's acclaimed Atkins Diet Program.

Atkins, at its peak, had more than thirty million Americans following the diet program. Twenty-percent of them polled said that they had been regularly purchasing Atkins and other low-carbohydrate products to support this diet. In fact, in 2003 alone, more than 3,000 new low-carbohydrate products were introduced to the market.

The Atkins diet phenomenon was marked by a rapid rise in popularity, and suffered the tell-tale rapid decline of a fad. Diets are generally referred to as "fad-to-franchise" products. This means they initially behave like a true fad, but rather than disappearing from the marketplace permanently, experience radical ups and downs of consumer demand.

As with most fads, "Atkins suffered extravagant success, followed by extravagant failure", and the July 2005 bankruptcy of Atkins Nutritionals signaled the official end of what some experts referred to as unrivalled food and diet marketing.

tip

Consumer taste(s) can create extravagant, rapid wealth and similarly prove disastrous with the rapidity in which consumers reject yesterday's standard(s). Plan accordingly and never stop observing evident trends.

This example illustrates that, in business, timing is everything. In franchising, however, product analysis is equally important. If a business is experiencing enormous success, but should be characterized properly as a fad, to then develop a franchise organization in order to distribute the business nationally would almost certainly prove fatal, once the fad cycle reaches its expected end.

who will help you manage your franchise?

Like a traditional business, the ability to attract and retain qualified personnel is important to franchising. Because franchising is an industry that not only provides a consumer demanded product or service, but also requires the knowledge and management of a distributed franchise network, it is important to find the right individuals, who have a capacity and competence, to help you manage both.

76

For example, in the early stages of your franchise development, you will likely rely on the same individual to handle your external consumer marketing, as well as your franchise recruitment marketing. While this may not be an ideal scenario for your franchise network, it is typically the kind of "multi-tasking" that many new Franchisors are forced to endure. Until the franchise grows, and available capital and resources become available to hire individuals with distinct specialties for marketing in each segment, it will likely remain a necessity for you to look to your staff to manage dual roles.

Being able to attract and retain high-quality staff will be a critically important factor for your franchise's success. Franchisees are somewhat creatures of habit. They become very accustomed to the internal contacts in the franchise network, and grow comfortable with those individuals. For this, it is important to hire a core staff that you feel will be available to your franchise for many years.

Additionally, when you start out in franchising, you yourself will be very new to the industry, and although it is likely that you will engage the services of a professional franchise development firm initially, you will still require experienced franchise executives to help you emerge as a serious contender. It is vital to make an attempt to hire individuals in your initial staffing that are accustomed to, and experienced in operating a franchise model.

77

Furthermore, it is important that you maintain at least one location or prototype facility for things such as prospective Franchisee tours, further product development, assessment of equipment and raw materials, training and testing. If you transition your existing key employees to the franchise entity, you may consequently leave your existing business vulnerable to having to hire new people, and compromising the quality of the delivery of the product or service from that original location.

Additionally, your original location must continue to be a model that not only produces earnings, but also continues to perfect product delivery and operational systemization. Reconsider the impact of allowing your existing employees to be transitioned into the franchise business entity before offering each the opportunity.

Also, if you plan to move or promote all or most of your existing staff, it is likely that many of the key Franchisor positions will be reserved for your existing workforce, which is assumed to have no experience in franchising. As mentioned, it is vital that the first key individuals bring some experience to the relationship as it is likely going to be a greater learning curve for you and your existing staff, to learn about franchising, than it will be for each new executive to learn about your business. Intentionally choosing to not consider outside experienced candidates will certainly have an impact on the growth rate of your franchise during the challenging early development phase.

CHAPTER 7

Choosing a Franchise Developer...Beware of Sharks

By the title of this chapter, it is evident that I have a sense of bitterness for some of the service providers that you may encounter as a business owner looking to develop your business into a franchise organization. Once you make the decision to franchise, you will begin the search for the service providers necessary to help you complete the necessary feasibility studies, structure your franchise offering, draft the necessary legal documents, prepare your franchise operations manuals, implement the necessary technology, and develop a sales and marketing plan for your franchise.

There are essentially three types of professional service providers that you should consider when looking for assistance with the franchise development process.

attorneys

The first is the Franchise Attorney. There is no doubt that there is a demanding legal requirement that must be fulfilled before your franchise is legally able to sell franchise units. An experienced franchise attorney is certainly a vital part of the process, and is a wealth of knowledge with reference to how to create and structure your Uniform Franchise Offering Circular (UFOC) properly, completely and in a manner that will minimize any future problems that you may have due to improper or incomplete preparation of this document.

Also, the Franchise Agreement, which is essentially an appendix and part of the Uniform Franchise Offering Circular, further declares and commits the Franchisor to provide certain services and obligations, and outlines the Franchisee obligations, along with the means for either party to enforce and/or obtain remedy, should either party fail to perform any or all of the commitments bound to in the Franchise Agreement.

Now, franchise attorneys are an excellent resource for the drafting and legal structuring of the documents themselves. They are clearly qualified, and skillfully trained, to prepare these documents for acceptance by the state regulatory agencies, and for meeting the Federal Trade Commission requirements for proper preparation of the UFOC.

As you perform a search for providers that offer franchise development services, you will surely find advertisements and offers by law firms and independent attorneys to complete these important documents. Many of them will have extensive franchise experience and limit their practice solely to the franchise practice area, providing them the specialization needed to anticipate and meet the specific requirements that you will encounter at many of the individual state levels, as well as handling most other nuances of the franchise regulatory process effectively. Not surprisingly, others will only occasionally dabble in franchise law, yet advertise their service offerings in this specialty.

82

Generally speaking, franchise attorneys will charge a typical firm rate of $200 to $350 per hour, for their legal services and the total billings for the preparation of these documents for your business can range anywhere from as low as $10,000 to $15,000, to as high as $100,000 to $150,000. I have seen pricing quoted just about anywhere between those highs and lows and there is no specific range for either an independent, or firm-based attorney pricing.

The drawback to limiting your reliance exclusively on attorneys for the development of your franchise, is that although they are an excellent and required resource to prepare the formal legal documents necessary for the sale of your franchise, they can be grossly lacking in their knowledge of specific business development and strategy elements that are critical to developing a successful franchise model.

While attorneys are clearly competent in their ability to draft binding and complete legal documents, unless you alone, or with the help of other professional business developers, have specifically determined how your franchise is structured, and what terms, conditions, costs and obligations will be required by all parties, much of the critical analysis and decision making may be lost, or incompetently determined solely by a franchise attorney.

tip

Before hiring a specific Attorney to solely franchise your business. Ask yourself; would I hire this Attorney to draft a legal document? And...would I hire this Attorney as a Management Consultant? If both answers are not "Yes", keep interviewing.

83

Fact is, while most attorneys make great legal service providers, few attorneys are capable of achieving great business intelligence, and are unable to confidently structure a business strategy as complex as a franchise, without a formal business education or direct industry experience. I am not suggesting that franchise attorneys have no or little business acumen, I am merely pointing out that while they spend numerous years perfecting their legal craft, it is important to be absolutely certain that executives with advanced business knowledge help determine how the franchise should be structured.

It is vital to take into consideration all the elements that impose a risk, such as competitive threats, industry trends, regulatory requirements, capitalization factors, markets cycles and other risks specific to an industry. I would recommend the use of a franchise attorney only in the case where you are certain that the business strategy and structure for your franchise has been analyzed and determined well in advance of the sole reliance on an attorney.

Franchise Attorneys should be used specifically, to prepare the required legal documents, look for weakness in the terms and conditions, declare usurious or otherwise unfair terms, identify material omissions, meet and anticipate regulatory requirements and advise you when there are issues that otherwise might cause objection or weaken your legal or regulatory position.

consultants

Franchise consultants or developers range from being highly competent, experienced and valuable, to being grossly neglectful and essentially fraudulent in their representations.

Franchise consultants that have based their specialty on the development of the franchise model can be an undisputable asset for a new Franchisor. Because franchising requires the knowledge and experience seldom available to an independent business owner, it pays to engage in the services of a thorough and reputable professional franchise development firm.

Franchising, if done correctly, can create an essentially eternal and perpetual business structure whose brands, products and reputation can long outlive its original founders. On the other hand, franchising done improperly and/or neglectfully, can prove disastrous, causing even the best business opportunity to fail.

In my opinion, franchise developers need to provide more than most do. If you were to question the top ten franchise development firms available for hire in the United States, it is my experience that a large majority of them would quote and claim to perform and complete all the key elements required to properly launch a new franchise offering.

However, all too often in the end, many franchise developers focus on a very short list of deliverables. When many franchise developers and franchise attorneys quote franchise development services, you will commonly find a similar focus in the negotiation(s). Because the Uniform Franchise Offering Circular (UFOC) is commonly presented to business owners as a significantly complex document, particularly when paired with the Franchise Agreement, many franchise service providers use that unfamiliarity to justify not only their service's singular value, but go on to quote excessively high development fees for their preparation.

Some things never change, and many franchise development firms have found that fear can elicit a response from most buyers that can be translated into higher prices and a greater sense of urgency. While I agree that the UFOC and Franchise Agreement are a vital and critical component of a properly developed franchise offering, I repeatedly urge you to remember and acknowledge that there are numerous other elements that together comprise the total franchise offering.

85

From a practical standpoint, achieving the legal requirements to allow the Franchisor to sell his franchise does not even begin to satisfy the other business necessities that will be mandatory for a Franchisor to confidently and effectively market and grow his franchise.

beware   It is recommended that any Consultant you consider has an advanced business education as well as franchise industry experience to offer true value. Having once "worked for a franchisor" is not adequate preparation to competently act as a business consultant.

As expected, other specific items, such as feasibility studies, market research, identity and messaging studies, territory assignments, demographic distributions, trademark and copyright protections, operations manuals and standards development, opening requirements, interior and exterior design specifics, and numerous other factors are vitally critical for a Franchisor to package and sell his franchise.

In my experience, having frequently seen through the eyes of my clients, and reviewed the final work product of many of the franchise developers in this country, it is clear that beyond the preparation of a largely boiler-plated UFOC and Franchise Agreement, there is little evidence that franchise developers are either capable of, or interested in equipping their clients with the tools, assets and resources that will be needed for them to sell their first franchise.

So, when you interview and research available franchise consulting firms, put them to the test. If they tell you that they will create an effective and compelling Franchisee recruiting package, ask for five samples. If they say that they will develop an online, web-based marketing strategy, ask for a live example of their work. If they claim to be marketing and branding experts, make them prove it by presenting a portfolio of their achievements and review the claimed "before and afters".

86

beware "One Stop Shops", promising to complete all the required consulting, legal, marketing and technology requirements for a new franchise are becoming more common, not by practice, but by empty promise. Ask for hard evidence of deliverable "claims" before proceeding with any consulting firm.

Reluctantly, in the franchise consulting business, there are far too many professional service providers, consultants and law firms, claiming to be "one-stop shops", but when pressed, have little more to show for their work than an endless stack of UFOCs.

Alternatively, if you are able to obtain live examples of marketing and other concept development work, examine it closely. If you find yourself looking for presumably different client representations and there is an awkward similarity in scope and content on the deliverables, then you know you have found yourself a service provider that has largely perfected the art of "find and replace". Not, coincidentally, it is the same skill many use in preparing the UFOC and franchise agreements as well.

The lesson here is that it is important to take the time to dig deeper when choosing a franchise developer. Sadly, it is not uncommon for franchise developers to provide you a laundry list of the service points and deliverables they will provide, but when put to the test, they are short on quality, short on results and in the worst-case, short on specific and tangible examples of their work.

Should this be the case, then it is likely if hired, that you are not going to emerge from the development process adequately prepared to offer your franchise. Furthermore, what deliverables you do get will commonly be completed last minute, lack professional expertise, be absent of any research based findings, or will unknowingly be completed by a third-party provider without any direct involvement or contribution by you.

In the right circumstances, and with the right team of professionals, franchise developers and consulting firms can accomplish a tremendous amount of work and bring a new Franchisor to a level of knowledge, competence and confidence in a very short period of time, as compared to a hiring an attorney solely.

Be sure and take the time to test the claims that a franchise developer or consultant is making. Although your insistence on their providing hard evidence to support the frequent "one stop shop" claims you will encounter, can be uncomfortable, move on from any provider who shrugs the request, or can't provide you with an impressive collection of legal, marketing, technology and sales deliverables for validation.

Your franchise concept may well be the most valuable asset you will ever develop. Take the time to thoroughly screen any "short list" providers before trusting your concept development to any firm.

sharks

The franchise industry, as with any industry that is experiencing rapid growth, has its share of either self-proclaimed professionals, service providers that have no long-term intentions of becoming experts in the industry, or flat out fraudulent firms or individuals that have absolutely no real-world franchising experience. These opportunists are created by virtue of a book they read, a seminar or two they attended or a commercial they watched where, with little reflection and professional or academic preparation, they decide that this industry has great potential and therefore they are going to become a player.

Many times, they begin by either fabricating or exaggerating their experience levels, and hope to find any business owner who is less qualified, or less capable of developing a franchise than they are, and with a little "technical UFOC talk", persuade the business owner that they are capable.

Frighteningly prevalent is a new trend that is increasing, whereby developers, whether established or not, insist that business owners grant them significant percentage ownership of the franchise entity, in order for them to take on the project, and effectively refuse to service the client unless they are willing to make them a partner in the new franchise.

This obviously means that if your franchise is successful and grows considerably, the percentage of the company that you have awarded while your franchise was still in its infancy, could be extremely valuable.

beware Be very wary of any Attorney, Consultant or Franchise Development Firm accepting equity or deferred compensation as payment for their development services. "Equity" developers are generally "one man" or underfunded firms that commonly abandon projects before completion, taking your franchise company's stock with them.

The obvious downside to choosing franchise developers who work for compensation other then the cash payment is that in most cases, the quality of their work is evaluated under far less scrutiny. Without a cash transaction, it becomes awkward for you as a business owner to insist, or reject work that is either lacking in quality or does not meet your expectations. Without an honest fee structure, it creates an imbalance between the owner and service provider relationship that, in almost every case, favors the service provider.

Additionally, you are now aware that it is critical as a new Franchisor, to go to market initially having all the resources required to compete and operate as a quality Franchisor. If franchise development services are compensated using equity or profit sharing methods, in most cases the service stops and the developer becomes reluctant to perform any services beyond the minimal requirements, which generally includes only the Uniform Franchise Offering Circular and Franchise Agreement.

Another form of unscrupulous deal making that you may encounter from franchise development service providers is the franchise now, pay me later, form of compensation. Put simply, this consists of a franchise developer offering to accept payment for their services from the first few franchise unit sales, once the franchise is developed.

For example, if their normal services would have cost $75,000 and your developed franchise is selling units for $25,000 each, then they will accept payment for their service after you have obtained the first three or more franchise buyers, and have received the franchise fee payments accordingly.

Because the scope of this book will not allow time to analyze the importance of choosing your new Franchisees carefully and cautiously, suffice it to say that as a new Franchisor, one of the biggest mistakes you can make is going to market, and immediately accepting investment from the first candidates that show an interest in your business and have the funds to purchase a franchise unit. A common, fatal mistake for new Franchisors is to quickly surround themselves with Franchisees, who are either unqualified, or unwilling to operate the franchise as is required.

Furthermore, having accepted unqualified Franchisees, you are then obligated to provide excessive support, training and management, along with increased risk, by accepting their payments, and awarding them a franchise. Fast-forward, and it is easy to imagine that your first ten, twenty or thirty Franchisees are largely unsuitable for your business, and now you are faced with the likelihood of either having disgruntled, non-productive or unqualified franchise owners, or running the risk of having Franchisees fail initially and tarnishing the success record for the franchise offering as a whole, which makes it nearly impossible to achieve sustained growth.

By agreeing to compensate a franchise developer with the payments from any number of initial franchise unit sales, you not only put your initial cash flow at risk by having to give a substantial amount of the first franchise fee payments to the developer, but you will also quickly find the developer's patience running thin if you choose to be selective with your first Franchisee applicants.

It is always better to find a reputable franchise development firm, work with them to obtain an affordable payment structure and pay for the services rendered in an honest and ethical way, than it is to rely on a creative compensation scheme in order to have someone fulfill your franchise development requirements.

going it alone

Lastly, let me point out the obvious option for completing your franchise development.

It is not written anywhere that you cannot go about developing your franchise on your own. I regularly speak to numerous business owners, who have obtained a significant amount of formal business education and practical business experience. Because the nature of effective franchise development is an extension of good business strategy, it is not impossible, and it is even probable that equipped with the right knowledge and experience, a business owner can develop his own franchise.

Now, I say this cautiously because a franchise is as different as a pizza parlor is from a rental car company. They are entirely different industries, based on an entirely different set of rules, regulations, risk factors and so forth. Jumping into franchising unassisted is like being a business owner who specializes in a particular industry, and then abruptly deciding to enter an entirely new industry without understanding the risks.

So, if you were to ask, "Why can't I just do this myself", I, or any reputable franchise developer, would say, "You can". The only requirements that would mandate that you use the services of

91

an outside provider, would be the final review of the UFOC and Franchise Agreement by an attorney and the auditing services of an accounting firm, to audit your company's financials in preparation of the UFOC.

Theoretically, you could familiarize yourself with the requirements and the disclosure that is necessary to adequately and completely prepare the UFOC, complete the exercise of assembling and drafting the documents, and as a final step, have an attorney provide the required review of the UFOC and Franchise Agreement. Bear in mind, however, that it is unlikely that you would be acting in a fiduciary capacity by attempting to develop your own legal documents, business structure and Franchise Operations Manuals, without relying on at least some professional outside, qualified resources.

In franchising, it is important to remember and maintain focus on the fact that in the end, when all the documents have been drafted, all the manuals have been written and the marketing plan executed, the logical next step will be to look for individuals and companies to invest directly into your business and purchase one or more franchise units. Imagine how you would feel as a buyer, if you found that the franchise you invested your hard-earned money into was developed largely by the business owner, lacking franchise knowledge, and using only limited expert guidance.

At the very least, if you attempt to develop your own franchise, you will likely miss out on critical key factors that, unknown to you, will have significantly affected the longevity and success of your franchise, or allowed you to avoid a potentially destructive risk factor. Any investment, and any business venture that has the potential to reward a business owner in the magnitude that a successful franchise can, deserves the proper commitment and investment to be certain that it is being developed and structured as professionally and appropriately as possible.

Finally, while initial research and a strong familiarization with the franchise industry, in general, is always recommended for any business owner that is contemplating franchising their business, it is strongly recommended that in one way or another, the business owner seeks out the highest level of professional services that can be afforded for the development of the business franchise.

CONCLUSION

I am hopeful that the previous pages have been rewarding, informational and effective in helping you personally find the answers you were seeking while exploring the option of franchising your business. The decision to franchise your business involves the consideration of numerous personal, financial and market factors, and prematurely venturing into this expansion option will likely increase your risk and anxiety. Reading this book is an excellent step in preparing yourself to confidently analyze your personal franchise risks and rewards.

When I entered the field of franchising, I never expected that the rewards, both personal and financial, would exceed my expectations in the magnitude that this industry has provided me. As a fellow entrepreneur, I am confident that if expansion of your business is in your strategic plans, it is unlikely any other expansion method would provide a more established, structured and accepted means to expand, all while significantly limiting your current business and personal financial risk(s).

While the scope of this publication is largely introductory, I invite you to contact me directly with any specific comments or questions you may have concerning the information presented here, or for assistance relating to a personal matter involving franchising. I can be reached anytime by emailing me at ralph@thefranchisebuilders.com, or by contacting me by telephone at the number listed on our website, found at http://www.thefranchisebuilers.com.

In closing, I wish you the best of luck with your personal business objectives, thank you for the confidence you bestowed upon me in reading my work and look forward to the possibility of becoming personally acquainted should you pursue franchising for your business, now or in the future.

APPENDIX A

acknowledgement

The following "live" Uniform Franchise Offering Circular is currently in use by our client GarageFloorCoating.com, a newly developed 2007 franchise, founded and owned by Rob Hanson of Phoenix, Arizona.

I would like to thank Rob for generously providing his company's regulatory UFOC for review in this book. Rob is a gifted business executive and a wonderful person, and we appreciate his business and friendship.

UNIFORM FRANCHISE OFFERING CIRCULAR

GARAGE FLOOR
coating franchise system inc.

**GARAGE FLOOR COATING
FRANCHISE SYSTEM, INC.**
A Nevada Corporation
3801 East Roeser Road, Suite #1
Phoenix, AZ 85040
(602) 579-2628 Phone
(602) 470-8040 Fax

BRIEF DESCRIPTION OF THE FRANCHISED BUSINESS

This Offering Circular describes a Garage Floor Coating single-unit franchise. The franchise will operate a Garage Floor Coating business and engage in the sale and application of floor coatings for residential and commercial customers and offer a variety of garage and storage products for sale. The franchise offering is referred to as a Garage Floor Coating "Business".

TOTAL AMOUNTS FROM ITEMS 5 AND 7

The initial fees payable to us for a franchise are $35,000 to $60,000, based on Territory size. The estimated initial investment for a franchise, including the initial fees, is $187,404 to $233,958.

RISK FACTORS

1. THE FRANCHISE AGREEMENT PERMITS YOU TO ARBITRATE OR LITIGATE WITH US ONLY IN MARICOPA COUNTY, ARIZONA. OUT-OF-STATE ARBITRATION OR LITIGATION MAY FORCE YOU TO ACCEPT A LESS FAVORABLE SETTLEMENT FOR DISPUTES. IT MAY ALSO COST MORE TO ARBITRATE OR LITIGATE WITH US IN ARIZONA THAN IN YOUR HOME STATE.

2. EVEN THOUGH THE FRANCHISE AGREEMENT STATES THAT ARIZONA LAW GOVERNS THE AGREEMENTS, LOCAL LAW MAY SUPERCEDE ARIZONA LAW IN YOUR STATE. PLEASE REFER TO ANY STATE-SPECIFIC ADDENDUM THAT MAY BE ATTACHED TO THIS OFFERING CIRCULAR FOR DETAILS.

3. CERTAIN PROVISIONS OF THE FRANCHISE AGREEMENT MAY BE SUPERSEDED BY STATE LAWS, WHICH PROVIDE YOU PROTECTION IN ADDITION TO YOUR RIGHTS AND REMEDIES UNDER THE FRANCHISE AGREEMENT. PLEASE REFER TO ANY STATE-SPECIFIC ADDENDUM THAT MAY BE ATTACHED TO THIS OFFERING CIRCULAR FOR DETAILS.

4. THE FRANCHISE AGREEMENT REQUIRES YOUR SPOUSE'S CONSENT AND BINDS YOUR SPOUSE, EVEN THOUGH YOUR SPOUSE MAY NOT BE INVOLVED IN THE FRANCHISED BUSINESS. THIS REQUIREMENT PLACES THE PERSONAL ASSETS OF OWNERS, SPOUSES AND FAMILY MEMBERS AT RISK.

5. THE ABILITY TO OPERATE A GARAGE FLOOR COATING FRANCHISE MAY REQUIRE YOU TO OBTAIN AND MAINTAIN STATE AND/OR OTHER REQUIRED LICENSURE. FAILURE TO DO SO MAY PROHIBIT YOU FROM OWNING OR OPERATING THIS BUSINESS NOW OR IN THE FUTURE.

6. THE FRANCHISOR RECENTLY BEGAN OFFERING FRANCHISES AND HAS NO HISTORY OF FRANCHISE OPERATIONS. YOU MAY WANT TO CONSIDER THIS IN DECIDING WHETHER TO PURCHASE A FRANCHISE.

7. THERE MAY BE OTHER RISKS CONCERNING THIS FRANCHISE.

Information comparing franchisors is available. Call the state administrators listed in Exhibit 1 or your public library for sources of information.

Registration of this franchise by a state does not mean that the state recommends, approves or endorses, or has verified the information in this Offering Circular. If you learn that anything in the offering circular is untrue, contact the Federal Trade Commission and your state agency listed in Exhibit 1.

The Issue Date of This Offering Circular is: October 20, 2006.

IN ACCORDANCE WITH THE REQUIREMENTS OF THE FEDERAL TRADE COMMISSION, THIS OFFERING CIRCULAR WAS ISSUED ON THE DATE SET FORTH ABOVE. THE EFFECTIVE DATE(S) OF THIS OFFERING CIRCULAR IN THE STATES OF CALIFORNIA, HAWAII, ILLINOIS, INDIANA, MARYLAND, MINNESOTA, NEW YORK, NORTH DAKOTA, RHODE ISLAND, SOUTH DAKOTA, VIRGINIA, WASHINGTON AND WISCONSIN, IF APPLICABLE, ARE LISTED IN EXHIBIT 7 OF THIS OFFERING CIRCULAR.

GARAGE FLOOR COATING FRANCHISE SYSTEM, INC.
A Nevada Corporation
3801 East Roeser Road, Suite #1
Phoenix, AZ 85040
(602) 579-2628 Phone
((602) 470-8040 Fax

INFORMATION FOR PROSPECTIVE FRANCHISEES
REQUIRED BY FEDERAL TRADE COMMISSION

TO PROTECT YOU, WE'VE REQUIRED YOUR FRANCHISOR TO GIVE YOU THIS INFORMATION. WE HAVEN'T CHECKED IT AND DON'T KNOW IF IT'S CORRECT. IT SHOULD HELP YOU MAKE A DECISION. STUDY IT CAREFULLY. WHILE IT INCLUDES SOME INFORMATION ABOUT YOUR CONTRACT, DON'T RELY ON IT ALONE TO UNDERSTAND YOUR CONTRACT. READ ALL OF YOUR CONTRACT CAREFULLY. BUYING A FRANCHISE IS A COMPLICATED INVESTMENT. TAKE YOUR TIME TO DECIDE. IF POSSIBLE, SHOW YOUR CONTRACT AND THIS INFORMATION TO AN ADVISOR, SUCH AS A LAWYER OR AN ACCOUNTANT. IF YOU FIND ANYTHING YOU THINK MAY BE WRONG OR ANYTHING IMPORTANT THAT'S BEEN LEFT OUT, YOU SHOULD LET US KNOW ABOUT IT. IT MAY BE AGAINST THE LAW.

THERE MAY BE LAWS ON FRANCHISING IN YOUR STATE. ASK YOUR STATE AGENCIES ABOUT THEM.

FEDERAL TRADE COMMISSION
WASHINGTON, D.C. 20580

Date of Issuance: October 20, 2006

IN ACCORDANCE WITH THE REQUIREMENTS OF THE FEDERAL TRADE COMMISSION, THIS OFFERING CIRCULAR WAS ISSUED ON THE DATE SET FORTH ABOVE. THE EFFECTIVE DATE(S) OF THIS OFFERING CIRCULAR IN THE STATES OF CALIFORNIA, HAWAII, ILLINOIS, INDIANA, MARYLAND, MINNESOTA, NEW YORK, NORTH DAKOTA, RHODE ISLAND, SOUTH DAKOTA, VIRGINIA, WASHINGTON AND WISCONSIN, IF APPLICABLE, ARE LISTED IN EXHIBIT 7 OF THIS OFFERING CIRCULAR.

APPENDIX A

TABLE OF CONTENTS

Exhibits to the GARAGE FLOOR COATING FRANCHISE SYSTEM, INC. Uniform Franchise Offering Circular

101

ITEM 1: THE FRANCHISOR, ITS PREDECESSORS AND AFFILIATES

To simplify the language in this Offering Circular, "We" or "Us" means GARAGE FLOOR COATING FRANCHISE SYSTEM, INC., the franchisor. "You" means the person who buys the franchise. The franchisee may be a person, corporation, or partnership. If the franchisee is a corporation, partnership or limited liability company, "you" does not include the principals of the corporation, partnership or limited liability company, unless otherwise stated.

The Franchisor, Its Predecessors and Affiliates

We are a Nevada corporation established on October 5, 2006 with a principal business address at 3801 East Roeser Road, Suite #1, Phoenix, AZ 85040. We do business only under our corporate name. There is no predecessor. We have one affiliate, Dexter Coatings, Inc. ("DCI"). We are offering franchises for the first time under this Offering Circular and we have never offered franchises in any other line of business. DCI operates one Business of the type being offered in this Offering Circular, the address of which are listed in Exhibit 3 of this Offering Circular. Our agent(s) for service of process are identified in Exhibit 2 of this Offering Circular.

DCI are under common control with GARAGE FLOOR COATING FRANCHISE SYSTEM, INC. DCI supplies our franchisees with the Retail and Construction Merchandise required to operate a Business and provides some Services. DCI also owns and operates a Business that offers the Services and sells the Merchandise, however, DCI will not operate in the Territory of a franchisee. DCI is an Arizona corporation and has been in business since 1996. The principal business address of DCI is 3801 East Roeser Road, Suite #1, Phoenix, AZ 85040.

The Franchisor's Business

We offer and sell Garage Floor Coating franchises. Under the Franchise Agreement (the "Franchise Agreement"), which is Exhibit 5 to this Offering Circular, we grant the franchisee the right to establish and operate a Garage Floor Coating Business at a single location (the "Business"). The Garage Floor Coating Business will engage in the sale and application of floor coatings for residential and commercial customers and offer a variety of garage and storage products for sale. The garage and storage products and accessories for sale are referred to collectively as the "Merchandise." The application and repair of floor coatings is referred to collectively as the "Service."

Garage Floor Coating Businesses are distinguished from other retail and construction businesses by their unique methods of product selection, uniform standards, specifications and procedures for operations, construction techniques, cost estimating and control, inventory and staffing, merchandising and marketing standards and procedures, quality and uniformity of products and services, employee training and assistance, and advertising and promotional programs, all of which we may change, improve, and further develop (the "System"). You will operate your Business under the service mark and trade name "Garage Floor Coating" and other trade names, trademarks and service marks that we specify now or designate for use in the future in connection with the System (collectively, the "Proprietary Marks").

Market and Competition

As a Garage Floor Coating franchisee, you will be offering your Service and Merchandise to the general public. This consists primarily of residential customers. Additionally, depending on geographic location, commercial property and home builders may have need for the services and merchandise you will be offering. Competitors include any company engaged in the business of selling the Service and Merchandise, and there is no known dominant floor coating company throughout the United States. **However, you may compete with competitors with substantial resources ranging from national chains offering similar floor coating and garage/storage related services and merchandise to local, highly established floor coating companies.**

102

Prior Business Experience of the Franchisor and Its Affiliates

GARAGE FLOOR COATING FRANCHISE SYSTEM, INC. does not conduct the type of business you would operate as a franchisee. DCI is engaged in the type of business you would operate as a franchisee. We have offered franchises for sale similar to the franchise offered in this Offering Circular since October 20, 2006. Neither GARAGE FLOOR COATING FRANCHISE SYSTEM, INC. nor DCI has ever offered franchises other than the type of franchises described in this Offering Circular.

Industry-Specific Regulations

You must be familiar with local, county, state and Federal laws which apply generally to the construction industry. These laws may include chemical and hazardous waste regulations, zoning, health and safety, insurance, labor and licensing. WE STRONGLY ADVISE THAT YOU CONSULT YOUR ATTORNEY AND LOCAL, STATE AND FEDERAL GOVERNMENT AGENCIES BEFORE SIGNING A GARAGE FLOOR COATING FRANCHISE AGREEMENT TO DETERMINE ALL LEGAL REQUIREMENTS THAT YOU MUST COMPLY WITH TO CONSIDER THEIR EFFECTS ON YOU AND COST OF COMPLIANCE. It is your, and only your, responsibility, on a continuous basis, to investigate and satisfy all local, county, state and federal laws, since they vary from place to place and change over time.

ITEM 2: BUSINESS EXPERIENCE

The following is a list of our directors, principal officers, and other executives who will have management responsibility relating to the franchises offered under this Offering Circular, and their principal occupations and employers during the past five years.

103

President and CEO: Rob Hanson

In 1996, Phoenix resident and entrepreneur Robert Hanson launched Southwest Resurfacing Inc., a company specializing in the polymer coating of concrete pool decks, car dealerships and garage floors. In 1998, Rob determined that there was a growing market in garage floor coating and decided to change the name to Dexter Coatings Inc., and established the division GarageFloorCoating.com with the intention of focusing 100% on consumers wishing to enhance the aesthetics of their garage floors. Rob's vision of a company that truly provides quality workmanship and outstanding customer satisfaction has been realized in Garage Floor Coating.com.

Chief Operating Officer: Rob Hanson
Mr. Hanson, is also the company's Chief Operating Officer and has held this position since inception.

Treasurer:
Mr. Hanson, is also the company's Treasurer and has held this position since inception.

Franchise Marketing Officer: Thad Flores

Mr. Flores started with Garage Floor Coatings.com in late 2005 as director of Franchise Development. From 2003 until 2005, Mr. Flores was an Assistant Vice President in residential lending with the National Bank of Arizona in Phoenix, Arizona. From 2002 until 2003, Mr. Flores was a Loan Officer with The Creative Mortgage Group in Scottsdale, Arizona. From 2001 until 2002, Mr. Flores was a Wholesale Loan Representative with Indy Mac Bank, FSB in Phoenix, Arizona. From 1991 until 2001, Mr. Flores was a Residential Real Estate Appraiser servicing various companies in Phoenix, Arizona and Honolulu, Hawaii. He earned an Associates Degree in Business from Phoenix Community College, Phoenix, AZ in 1982, followed by two years of Construction Management training at Arizona State University, Tempe, AZ.

Franchise Broker: Philip Liddell, President, Franchise Industries, LLC

Mr. Philip Liddell will be acting as a sales broker for Garage Floor Coating Franchise System and will be under the indirect supervision of Garage Floor Coating Franchise System management. He will be acting in a limited sales capacity to assist the company with prospect qualification and review and will be compensated directly from the company. He has been acting as an independent franchise broker since 2003 and previously held numerous senior sales and marketing positions. He earned a Bachelor of Science in Marketing from University of Southern New Hampshire in 1998.

ITEM 3: LITIGATION

No litigation is required to be disclosed in this Offering Circular.

ITEM 4: BANKRUPTCY

No corporation or person previously identified in Items 1 or 2 of this Offering Circular has been involved as a debtor in proceedings under the U.S. Bankruptcy Code required to be disclosed in this Item 4.

ITEM 5: INITIAL FRANCHISE FEE

Upon your submission of a Garage Floor Coating Franchisee Application, you must pay us an application fee of $500.00 and a franchise fee of $34,500, for a total of $35,000 for (1) one territory; or an application fee of $500.00 and a franchise fee of $59,500, for a total of $60,000 for (2) two territories. The franchise fee is uniform as to all franchisees, is deemed fully earned upon payment, and, in consideration of administrative and other expenses we incur in granting this franchise and for our lost or deferred opportunity to enfranchise others, is nonrefundable under any circumstances, except where we do not approve your application for a franchise, where we will refund your paid franchise fee, less $500 (five-hundred dollars), which we will retain as an application administrative fee, within 15 days. We will not give refunds for any other reason. You will have (6) six months from the opening of your business to begin doing business in your second territory. Prior to conducting business in your second territory, you will be required to purchase additional equipment and materials, and hire employees. The investment will be the same as will be required to be open for business in your first territory.

ITEM 6: OTHER FEES

The following table describes other recurring or isolated fees or payments that you must pay to us, or which we impose or collect on behalf of a third party, in whole or in part in connection with the operation of a single Garage Floor Coating Business. Unless otherwise indicated below, all of the fees listed below are imposed by, payable to and collected by us and are nonrefundable.

NAME OF FEE	AMOUNT	DUE DATE	REMARKS
Royalty Fee	6.5% of Gross Sales	The 15th of each month	See Note 1
Advertising Fund Contributions	Up to 1% of your Gross Sales	The 15th of each month	See Note 2
Local Advertising and Administration Fee	Up to 9% of your Gross Sales	The 15th of each month	See Note 3
Initial Local Advertising	Up to $10,000	As incurred	See Note 4
Initial Inventory	$34,500	Before beginning operation of the Business	See Note 5

Administrative Services Fee	1% of Gross Sales	The 15th of each month	See Note 6
Reserve Account Fee	$10,000	Before beginning operation of the Business	See Note 7
Manager Training Fee	$250 per day of training or then-current training fee	As incurred	See Note 8
Additional Training Fee	$250 per day of training or then-current training fee	As incurred	See Note 9
Seminar	Cost of attendance	As incurred	See Note 10
Insurance	Cost of insurance. If you fail to maintain your insurance as required, there is an 18% administrative cost if we exercise our right to procure your insurance	As required by insurer or broker	See Note 11
Supplier Approval/ Testing Costs	Up to $1,000	As incurred	See Note 12
Collection Costs, Attorneys' Fees, Interest	The greater of (i) $100; or (ii) the fees we incur; plus interest at 18% or highest lawful interest rate for commercial transactions	As incurred	See Note 13
Books and Records	Cost of audit and/or inspection.	As required	See Note 14
Financial Records and Reports	Cost of preparing financial statements	Annually	See Note 15
Taxes on Payments to Us	Amount of tax or assessment	When imposed by taxing authority	See Note 16
Indemnification	Amount of claim or judgment	As incurred	See Note 17
Renewal Fee	$5,000	Before renewal	See Note 18
Transfer Fee	$5,000	Upon transfer	See Note 19

105

Note 1: Royalty Fee. You must pay us a royalty fee of 6.5% of the previous month's Gross Sales of your Business. For purposes of the royalty fee, "Gross Sales" includes all revenues you generate from all business conducted by your Business or in and from your business during the preceding reporting period, including amounts you received whether from cash sales or charged sales of services and products, or otherwise, or revenues from any source arising out of the operation of the Business, including any proceeds of any business interruption insurance paid to you with respect to your Business, less all returns, refunds and allowances, if any. "Gross Sales" do not include the amount of any tax imposed by any federal, state, municipal or other governmental authority; you agree to pay these amounts as and when due.

Note 2: Advertising Fund Contributions. We may establish a national advertising fund ("National Fund") for the common benefit of franchisees. We may also establish regional advertising funds ("Regional Fund(s)") for the benefit of System franchisees whose Businesses are located within designated regions. We have the right to require you to participate in and contribute monthly to either or both funds, a total amount not to exceed 1% of your monthly Sales. See Item 11 of this Offering Circular for more details regarding advertising funds. We will collect the advertising fund contributions by deducting the amount due from your Commission each month, or at such other time and in such other manner as we may designate.

Cooperative advertising allowances from Suppliers and other parties will be used at our sole discretion and do not reduce your advertising fund obligations.

Note 3: Local Advertising and Administration Fee. In addition to the advertising fund contributions described above, you must pay us up to a total amount not to exceed 9% of your monthly Sales per month that we will use to advertise your Business and for our cost to administer the local advertising activities ("Local Advertising and Administration Fee"), and up to $10,000 for initial local advertising in conjunction with your Business's grand opening ("Initial Local Advertising"). The amount you must pay may change monthly depending on the number of Business in your market that pay the Local Advertising and Administration Fee. In addition, we may, at our sole discretion, increase the Local Advertising and Administration Fee annually by an amount not to exceed 10% of the then current Local Advertising and Administrative Fee amount. Should we deem it necessary to increase the Local Advertising and Administration Fee beyond the current monthly maximum of 9% of your monthly Sales, we will provide written notice at least 30 days prior to the increase.

If we do not establish a National or Regional Advertising Fund, as described in Note 2 above, we may require you to expend an additional amount not to exceed 1% of your monthly Sales on local advertising in addition to the Local Advertising and Administration Fee. We will collect the Local Advertising and Administration Fees by deducting the amount due from your Sales each month, or at such other time and in such other manner as we may designate.

Cooperative advertising allowances from Suppliers and other parties will be used at our sole discretion and do not reduce your local advertising obligations.

Note 4: Initial Local Advertising. In addition to the advertising fees described above, you must pay us up to $10,000 for initial local advertising in conjunction with your Business's grand opening ("Initial Local Advertising"). The amount you must pay will be determined by a number of factors, such as the location of your Business and the media rates for your market. We will notify you of the cost of your initial local advertising and you must pay us the amount owed prior to our incurring these costs. (See Items 7 and 11 for more information on Initial Local Advertising.)

Cooperative advertising allowances from Suppliers and other parties will be used at our sole discretion and do not reduce your local advertising obligations.

106

Note 5: Initial Inventory. You must purchase all Merchandise and Equipment from DCI or another approved supplier as we designate. Such purchases will represent 100% of your overall purchases of such items. At the time that we designate and before your Business begins operations, you will pay us a sum of $32,600 for the purchase of initial inventory for your Business, and you will be required to purchase locally, equipment and supplies in the amount of approximately $1,900 for a total initial inventory purchase of approximately $34,500. You must at all times maintain sufficient levels of inventory to adequately meet consumer demand. After your Business's opening, we will deduct (30%) of your gross sales which will be deposited into an inventory replenishment account and used to purchase additional inventory for your Business as needed. When the inventory replenishment account reaches ($30,000), we will not deduct any additional funds until inventory is repurchased utilizing the funds from the inventory replenishment account.

Note 6: Administrative Services Fee. You must pay us an Administrative Services Fee of 1% of your Gross Sales. For this fee we will provide your Business with select administrative, operational, customer service and sales related services from our corporate office or from a location of our designation. We reserve the right to add or discontinue specific services offering(s) and will notify you within 60 days of such changes. Participation in our service offerings is mandatory. At the time of this writing we will provide unlimited inbound call management for your business, which may include introducing prospects to the available GFC products and services, quoting non-binding verbal pricing estimates, message taking and contact to you and your staff regarding service requests and other general customer service related tasks as determined by our available resources and prospects/customer requests. We reserve the right to increase the Administrative Services Fee beyond the current monthly amount and we will provide written notice at least 60 days prior to the increase. Additionally, we reserve the right to transfer some or all of the service(s) performance to a vendor or supplier, terminate the offering of this franchisee service(s), and cancel the fee requirement and will provide you with written notice at least 60 days prior should be exercise any of these option(s).

Note 7: Reserve Account. We require that you maintain a $10,000.00 Reserve Account with us in the event that your business receives legal monetary claims against it for application and/or repair work uncompleted or otherwise claimed against, or to compensate us for unpaid inventory/materials charges. We will return this money to you six months following the sale, transfer or termination of your Business, less any claims paid. We reserve the right to determine and pay claims exclusively using this Reserve Account.

Note 8: Manager Training Fee. At your request and subject to the availability of our personnel, we will train you and/or your additional or replacement managers at a cost to you of $250 per day of training or the then-current training fee in addition to other costs and expenses, including travel and living expenses.

Note 9: Additional Training Fee. At your request and subject to the availability of our personnel, we will train you and/or your additional or replacement managers at a cost to you of $250 per day of training or the then-current training fee in addition to other costs and expenses, including travel and living expenses.

Note 10: Seminar Costs. We may periodically organize company-wide seminars and conferences and require that you or one of your managers attend each seminar. You are responsible for all costs of attendance, including travel, lodging, meals and other personal expenses.

Note 11: Insurance. During the term of the Franchise Agreement, you must obtain and maintain at your expense comprehensive general liability insurance covering product and automobile liability, personal injury and property damage coverage in the amounts we prescribe. See Item 8 of this Offering Circular for information about our insurance requirements. If you fail to comply with our minimum insurance requirements, we have the right to obtain and maintain the requisite insurance coverage at your sole expense for which you must pay us the premium cost of the insurance plus an administrative cost equal to 18% of the cost for obtaining insurance on your behalf. We have the right to increase or otherwise modify the minimum insurance requirements upon 30-days' prior written notice to you, and you must comply with any such modification within the time specified in the notice.

107

Note 12: Supplier Approval/Testing Costs. If we incur any costs in connection with testing a particular product or evaluating a supplier at your request, you must reimburse us our reasonable testing costs, regardless of whether we subsequently approve the supplier. We estimate such to cost up to $1,000. See Item 8 of this Offering Circular for more information about designated and approved suppliers.

Note 13: Collection Costs, Attorneys' Fees, Interest. You must pay us a late fee in the amount of not less than $100 per incident for any late payment or underpayment of the royalty or advertising fee, and any other charges or fees you owe us or our affiliates. Additionally the outstanding amount will bear interest from the due date until paid at the lesser of 18% interest per year or the highest lawful interest rate, which we may charge for commercial transactions in the state in which your Business is located. If you are in breach or default of any monetary or non-monetary material obligation under the Franchise Agreement or any related agreement between you and us and/or our affiliates, and we or our affiliates engage an attorney to enforce our respective rights (whether or not we initiate formal judicial proceedings), you must pay all reasonable attorneys' fees, court costs and litigation expenses we or our affiliates incur. If you institute any legal action to interpret or enforce the terms of the Franchise Agreement, and your claim is denied or the action is dismissed, you must reimburse us our reasonable attorneys' fees, and all other reasonable costs and expenses incurred in defending against the action. We are entitled, under the Franchise Agreement, to have this amount awarded as part of the judgment in the proceeding.

Note 14: Books and Records. If any audit reveals any royalties due on Gross Sales that were not reported and paid or any other amounts due, you will immediately pay us twice the royalty that we would have received had the Gross Sales amount(s) been reported and/or the other amounts due, plus interest from the date when the royalties and/or other payments should have been submitted. Additionally, you must pay us the reasonable cost of the audit and/or inspection, including the cost of outside auditors and attorneys, if we incur these costs. The remedies stated in this section will not be our sole remedy in such situations. Franchisee will be considered in default of the Agreement and we will be entitled to all other remedies applicable on default by Franchisee.

Note 15: Financial Records and Reports. You must have prepared and maintain annual financial reports and operating statements in the form we specify, prepared by a Certified Public Accountant or state-licensed public accountant, within 90 days after the close of each of your fiscal years.

Note 16: Taxes on Payments to Us. If any taxing authority, wherever located, imposes any future tax, levy or assessment on any payment you make to us, in addition to all payments due us, you must pay the tax, levy or assessment.

Note 17: Indemnification. You must defend, indemnify and hold us harmless from all fines, suits, proceedings, claims, demands, obligations or actions of any kind (including costs and reasonable attorneys' fees) arising in whole or in part from the operation of your Business, including your advertising, except as otherwise provided in the Franchise Agreement.

Note 18: Renewal Fee. If you wish to exercise your right to renew the Franchise Agreement, you must pay us a renewal fee of $5,000. Each renewal period is effective for 10 years.

Note 19: Transfer Fee. We have the right to condition the proposed sale or transfer of the Franchised Business or of your interest in the Franchised Business upon your payment of a $5,000 transfer fee.

ITEM 7: YOUR ESTIMATED INITIAL INVESTMENT

Except as otherwise described in the notes below, the following table provides an estimate of your initial investment and the costs necessary to begin operating under the Franchise Agreement for a Garage Floor Coating Business. Actual costs will vary for each franchise depending on a number of factors, including market condition, the geographic location of your Business, the needed commercial equipment and vehicles, and the amount of construction work necessary for build-out of your Business's physical space. All fees and payments are nonrefundable unless otherwise stated or permitted by the payee.

DESCRIPTION OF EXPENSE	ESTIMATED COST LOW	ESTIMATED COST HIGH	METHOD OF PAYMENT	WHEN DUE	TO WHOM PAID
Initial Franchise Fee[1]	$35,000	$60,000	Lump sum	At signing of the Franchise Agreement	Us
Lease Deposit[2]	$500	$1,500	Lump sum	At signing of lease	Storage/Trailer Facility
Leasehold Improvements[3]	$0	$5,000	As incurred	As incurred	Contractor(s)
Office Furniture[4]	$750	$1,100	As incurred	As incurred	Third-party supplier(s)
Office Supplies and Equipment[5]	$600	$900	As incurred	Upon negotiated terms	Third-party supplier(s)
Computer System[6]	$2,783	$3,883	As incurred	As incurred	Us
Promotional Materials[7]	$500	$1,500	Lump sum	Before beginning operation of the Business	Third-party supplier(s)
Initial Local Advertising[8]	$8,000	$10,000	As incurred	As incurred	Us
Contractors License, Permits and other Licenses[9]	$2,000	$3,000	As incurred	As incurred	Governmental authorities
Training Expenses[10]	$2,500	$3,500	As incurred	As incurred	Hotels, restaurants, etc.
Prepaid Insurance Premium[11]	$300	$1,500	Lump sum	As incurred	Insurance carrier/broker
Telephones, Internet, Merchant Fees[12]	$1,415	$1,915	Lump sum	As incurred	Utility and telephone companies
Legal Costs[13]	$1,000	$2,000	As incurred	As incurred	Attorneys and government

					authorities
Initial Inventory and Shipping[14]	$34,750	$36,300	Lump Sum	Before beginning operation of the Business	Us
Reserve Account Fee[15]	$10,000	$10,000	Lump Sum	Before beginning operation of the Business	Us
Website Development Fee [16]	$500	$500	Lump Sum	Prior to opening	Third Party Supplier(s)
Working Capital (Cash)[17]	$20,000	$20,000	Lump Sum	Before beginning operation of the Business	Your bank account
Box Truck, Signage and Registration[18]	$ 49,500	$54,000	Lump Sum or Lease (OAC)	Before beginning operation of the Business	Auto Dealer / Private Party
Other Field Equipment[19]	$17,306	$17,360	Lump Sum	Before beginning operation of the Business	Us
TOTAL COSTS[20]	$187,404	$233,958			

Note 1. See Item 5 of this Offering Circular for a description of the initial franchise fee.

Note 2. At a minimum, in order to operate the business, it is necessary to lease or buy a climate-controlled storage facility, approximately 400 square feet in size, for storage of your application materials. You will also need to rent a space to store your truck outside of business hours. In some cases you may need to lease a small warehouse and secure a location to store your truck. Costs will vary depending available space and regulatory issues.

Note 3. The range in this category reflects an estimate for layout and construction build-out costs for a complete Garage Floor Coating Business. Your cost for leasehold improvements will vary depending upon the size of your Business and its geographic location. If you are converting an existing business into a Garage Floor Coating Business, your costs may be higher or lower depending on the available assets, fixtures and conversion costs. Construction costs in some areas of the country may exceed these estimates.

Note 4. The range in this category reflects an estimate for the cost of purchasing furniture for your Business.

Note 5. The range in this category reflects the estimated cost of purchasing equipment, including office supplies, and other office equipment to begin Business operations.

Note 6. You must purchase a computer system from our designated supplier prior to opening your Business. The computer system will include the hardware and software necessary to operate your Business and manage the sales, application and servicing areas of your business.

Note 7. Before you begin operating your Business, you will order promotional products for use in your business, such as labels, pens and other supplies with the Garage Floor Coating logo printed on them.

Note 8. Your Initial Local Advertising costs will depend on the media available in your local market and the rates charged for advertising in the available media. Prior to your Business's opening, we will develop your initial local advertising plan and notify you of the estimated cost, which you will pay to us. We will then contract with local media and carry out the advertising plan.

Note 9. You may be required to secure a contractors license before you begin your business. The cost of permits and licenses will depend upon the fees charged by your local municipality, county, state and licensing authority.

Note 10. Our estimate includes lodging accommodations and dining expenses for one person. Our estimate does not include expenses associated with traveling to our headquarters for offsite, classroom training. Your travel expenses, if any, will depend upon the distance of travel, mode of transportation, and the time of year in which your training occurs.

Note 11. Business insurance coverage will vary from state to state and will depend upon your prior loss experience, if any, and/or the prior loss experience of your insurance carrier in the state or locale in which you operate the business, and national or local market conditions. Insurance Carriers and brokers typically require a down payment equal to one quarter of the annual insurance payment and monthly payments of the remaining balance. See Item 8 of this Offering Circular for more information on insurance requirements.

Note 12. The range in this category reflects our estimates for telephone, Internet access services and merchant fees and equipment setup. We will require that you use the vendor of our choice for merchant, internet, wireless computer, and cellular telephone services.

Note 13. You may operate the Business as an individual, or you may transfer the Franchise Agreement to a corporation, partnership, or limited liability company. If you elect to operate the Business through a corporation or limited liability company, we estimate this will be your legal fees and state filing fees relating to forming the corporation or limited liability company.

Note 14. The range in this category reflects our estimate of the cost for the initial inventory required to adequately stock Materials in your Business prior to your Business's opening. Shipping costs will vary depending on your location.

Note 15. We require that you maintain a $10,000.00 Reserve Account with us in the event that your business receives legal monetary claims against it for application and/or repair work uncompleted or otherwise claimed against, or to compensate us for unpaid inventory/materials charges. We will return this money to you six months following the sale, transfer or termination of your Business, less any claims paid. We reserve the right to determine and pay claims exclusively using this Reserve Account.

Note 16. We have established a Website that will include a zip locator and a link to your personal Garage Floor Coating Franchise Website (your "Sitelet"). See Item 11 of this Offering Circular for additional information about our Website. Your Sitelet will include information relating to your specific business location and select content that we provide from our Website. Your Sitelet will also showcase the Garage Floor Coating products and services. We require that you use the supplier designated in the Manual to establish your Sitelet. You may not establish or maintain any other Website or engage in any other electronic marketing of products or services without our prior written approval. We reserve the right to change the requirements relating to your Sitelet at any time. You are also required to pay a monthly Website maintenance fee to the supplier that provides Website maintenance services. Currently, we estimate that the Website maintenance fee will not exceed $50 per month.

Note 17. You are required to have a minimum of $20,000 on hand prior to your Business's opening to be used as working capital and to cover initial operating expenses, including payroll. This figure is for an owner-operated Business with no owner's draw or salary. We cannot guarantee that you will not have additional expenses starting and operating your business. Your costs will depend on such factors as the extent to which you follow our methods and procedures, your management skill, experience and business acumen, local economic conditions, the local market for the Service and Merchandise, the prevailing wage rate, competition, the sales level reached during the initial period and occupancy costs for your Business. You must provide verification of available cash on hand by means of a bank statement or other similar documentation that meets our satisfaction.

Note 18. We have relied on the experience of the Business owned by DCI to complete these estimates. **You should review these figures carefully with a business advisor before making any decision to purchase the franchise.**

Note 19. The range in this category reflects the estimated cost of purchasing field equipment that will be provided by DCI.

110

Note 20. We have relied on the experience of the Business owned by DCI to complete these estimates. **You should review these figures carefully with a business advisor before making any decision to purchase the franchise.**

ITEM 8: RESTRICTIONS ON SOURCES OF PRODUCTS AND SERVICES

You must offer for sale in your Business all Merchandise, Equipment, Parts and Chemicals and only those specified by us. You must purchase all of the Merchandise, Equipment, Parts and Chemicals used in your Business from DCI or another approved vendor as specified by us. DCI may derive revenue from these purchases equal to the difference between the cost at which the items are purchased and the cost at which the items are sold to you.

You must purchase all inventory, equipment, fixtures and uniforms from us or our designated or approved suppliers. You must also purchase and use computer equipment and software that meets our standards and specifications from a vendor of our choice. Additionally, we have the right to establish designated and approved suppliers for other products and services offered in connection with the operation of your Business.

All required purchases are essential for building a positive image for the System and for individual sales growth. All required purchases must meet our standards and specifications. We formulate and modify our standards and specifications for products and services based upon the collective experience of our franchisees and affiliates. Our standards and specifications are described in the Franchise Agreement, the Operations Manual, and other written documents. We have the right, under the Franchise Agreement, to change the standards and specifications applicable to operation of the franchise, including standards and specifications for signs, furnishings, supplies, fixtures, inventory and equipment by written notice to you or through changes in the Operations Manual. You recognize that you may incur an increased cost to comply with these changes at your own expense; however, no change will materially alter your fundamental rights under the Franchise Agreement. We will notify you of any change to our standards and specifications by way of written amendments to the Operations Manual or otherwise in writing.

111

You must purchase and maintain insurance in the amounts we prescribe. We currently require our franchisees to maintain general commercial liability insurance with at least $2,000,000 in general aggregate coverage, $2,000,000 in product aggregate coverage, $1,000,000 for each occurrence, $1,000,000 for medical payments, $1,000,000 in personal injury coverage, $1,000,000 in Workers' Compensation coverage and business interruption insurance and automobile insurance coverage must include coverage for the business with a Combined Single Limit ("CSL") of $1,000,000. You must purchase auto insurance for your company vehicles which will include collision and comprehensive coverage as well as liability in the minimum amount of five hundred thousand dollars ($500,000) or the minimum required by state regulations, whichever is greater. Insurance carriers must be approved by us in advance and in writing. If your Lease requires you to purchase and maintain higher insurance limits, your Lease requirements will control. All insurance must be placed with a reputable insurance company licensed to do business in the state in which the Business is located and have a Financial Size Category equal to or greater than IX and Policyholders Rating of "A+" or "A" (Excellent) as assigned by Alfred M. Best and Company, Inc.

We, and our affiliates, may derive revenue from your required purchases. You will not receive any material benefit from purchasing from approved or designated suppliers. There are currently no purchasing or distribution cooperatives in existence for the Garage Floor Coating System.

The person you employ to maintain your books of account is subject to approval by us unless such person is a Certified Public Accountant.

ITEM 9: FRANCHISEE'S OBLIGATIONS

THIS TABLE LISTS YOUR PRINCIPAL OBLIGATIONS UNDER THE FRANCHISE AGREEMENT. IT WILL HELP YOU FIND MORE DETAILED INFORMATION ABOUT YOUR OBLIGATIONS IN THE FRANCHISE AGREEMENT AND IN OTHER ITEMS OF THIS OFFERING CIRCULAR.

OBLIGATION	SECTION IN THE FRANCHISE AGREEMENT	ITEM IN THE OFFERING CIRCULAR
a. Site selection and acquisition/lease	Sections 1.2 and 7.1	Items 7 and 11
b. Pre-opening purchases/leases	Section 7.5	Items 7, 8 and 11
c. Site development and pre-opening requirements	Sections 7.1 to 7.4	Items 6, 7 and 11
d. Initial and ongoing training	Section 7.3 and 8	Items 6, 7 and 11
e. Opening	Section 7.4	Item 11
f. Fees	Section 3	Items 5 and 6
g. Compliance with policies and Operations Manual	Sections 6.6 and 7.5	Items 8 and 11
h. Trademarks and proprietary information	Sections 4 and 5	Items 13 and 14
i. Restrictions on products and services offered	Section 7.6	Items 8 and 16
j. Warranty and customer service requirements	Section 7.7.2	Not Applicable
k. Territorial development and sales quotas	Section 1.4	Item 12
l. Ongoing product and service purchases	Section 7.5	Item 8
m. Maintenance, appearance and remodeling	Section 7.18	Item 11
n. Insurance	Section 9	Items 6, 7 and 8
o. Advertising	Section 10	Items 6, 7 and 11
p. Indemnification	Section 11.2	Item 6
q. Owner's participation, management and staffing	Section 7.7.5	Items 11 and 15
r. Records and reports	Section 3.5	Item 6
s. Inspections and audits	Sections 3.5.4	Item 11
t. Transfer	Section 12	Item 17
u. Renewal	Section 2.2	Item 17
v. Post-termination obligations	Section 15	Item 17
w. Non-competition covenants	Sections 16	Item 17
x. Dispute resolution	Section 17	Item 17
y. Usage of Internet for marketing	Section 6.11	Item 11

You must personally guaranty your obligations to us and DCI.

ITEM 10: FINANCING ARRANGEMENTS

We are unable to estimate whether or not you will be able to obtain financing for all or any part of your investment, and, if you are able to obtain financing, we cannot predict the terms of this financing. We will not guaranty your note, lease or other obligations. However, we will provide information regarding third party options to you, including at our discretion in the future, equipment leasing, and 401K rollover options. If you choose to utilize any of the lenders we introduce, we may receive a fee for our role in the process. It is your responsibility and ultimate decision with respect to the financing of your business.

ITEM 11: FRANCHISOR'S OBLIGATIONS

Except as described below, we need not provide any assistance to you pursuant to the Franchise Agreement:

Pre-Opening Obligations

Before you open your Business, we will perform the following obligations:

1. If you elect to establish an Operations Office outside of your home, we, or our designee, will review proposed sites for the location of your Business. We will use our best efforts to approve or disapprove your proposed site within 30 days from the date you submit your proposal along with all other information relating to the site that we may require. Upon the selection of a mutually acceptable site, we, or our designee, will review your lease and, at your request, offer you assistance and advice (see Section 6.2 of the Franchise Agreement). If you do not locate a mutually acceptable site and open for business within 160 days from the date we sign the Franchise Agreement, we have the right to terminate the Franchise Agreement and will be entitled to keep the initial franchise fee paid by you (see Sections 7.4 and 14.3.2 of the Franchise Agreement).

2. We will provide initial tuition-free training for a total of two individuals. We will train additional persons at a tuition rate of $2,500 for up to two-person training sessions so long as this person(s) attends training with you. You, if you are an individual (or at least one of your partners, shareholders or members if you are a partnership, corporation or limited liability company), must attend and complete the initial training program to our satisfaction (see Sections 6.4 and 8.1 of the Franchise Agreement). This initial training program consists of at least 10 days of classroom and on-the-job training at our headquarters or an affiliate-owned Business or other designated location, and three days of additional training at your Approved Location. This training program includes training in the operation and management of a Business, including methods and procedures to operate the Business, execute the application services portions of the business and promote merchandise sales, along with record keeping procedures, personnel management, inventory control, job costing, job estimating, trade hiring, scheduling, marketing & sales, warranty work and more. Your additional and/or replacement managers are not required to attend this initial training program, so long as this person(s) is trained by a person who has completed our initial training program. At your request, and subject to the availability of our personnel, we will train your additional and/or replacement managers at our then-current tuition, which is currently $2,500 per person.

4. We will supply you with the initial materials inventory for your Business, contingent on you paying us up to $32,600 for the cost of such inventory. In addition, you will be required to purchase locally, equipment and supplies in the amount of approximately $1,900 for a total initial inventory purchase of approximately $34,500. We will advise you with respect to merchandising and retailing, and other business, operational and advertising matters that directly relate to the franchise operation (see Section 6.5 of the Franchise Agreement).

5. We will develop an initial local advertising campaign for your Business and provide you with the estimated cost of the campaign, not to exceed $10,000. Prior to your Business's opening and after we receive your payment of the estimated cost, we will execute the campaign on your behalf (see Sections 6.6 and 10.4 of the Franchise Agreement).

6. We will loan you one copy of an operations and procedures manual, and appropriate revisions as may be made from time to time, referred to collectively as the "Operations Manual" (see Section 6.7 of the Franchise Agreement). Before you purchase the franchise, you may view the Operations Manual at our headquarters or elsewhere as arranged with us. We will not send our Operations Manual to either you or your attorney, and you may not copy or make notes regarding any portion of the Operations Manual. To protect the confidentiality of the Operations Manual, you must sign a confidentiality agreement in the form attached as Exhibit 6 to this Offering Circular before viewing the Operations Manual.

Post-Opening Obligations

After opening your Business and during the term of the Franchise Agreement, we will perform the following obligations:

1. We will provide, either ourselves or through our designee, periodic assistance as we deem appropriate and advisable at no additional charge to you. Subject to availability of personnel and at your request, we will make available corporate personnel to provide additional onsite or electronic assistance (at our sole discretion) at no additional charge to you (see Section 6.9 of the Franchise Agreement).

2. In addition to the assistance rendered to you before opening and in connection with the grand opening, we will provide you continuing consultation and advice as we deem advisable during the term of the Franchise Agreement, regarding personnel development and other business and operational matters that directly relate to the franchise operation at no additional charge to you. We will provide this assistance, at our option, either electronically or through onsite assistance by our appropriate personnel and/or other methods (see Section 6.9 of the Franchise Agreement).

3. We may, at our sole discretion, hold a mandatory annual conference at our headquarters or at a location we determine, no more than once per year, which will last approximately one to three days. We will determine the topics and agenda of the annual conference, which generally will include updating our franchisees on new developments affecting them, and exchanging information between our franchisees and our personnel concerning the operations and programs of the System. You must pay all costs and expenses to attend the annual conference (see Section 6.10 of the Franchise Agreement).

4. We will administer and manage your local advertising campaigns and notify you of the amount of your exact monthly local advertising expenditures.

5. You agree to repair, refinish, repaint, replace, and/or otherwise redo the Business Location or Equipment should the condition become compromising to the Image of the business and the franchise System brand. You agree that we have the right to direct you to remodel, re-equip, and otherwise refurbish the Franchised Business Premises in the manner necessary to bring it into conformance with other franchises of the type we and our franchisees are opening at the time of such direction.

114

Training Programs

Our initial training program is mandatory for all new franchisees prior to your Business's opening, and will take place at corporate headquarters. Training will be provided by or under the supervision of Rob Hanson or designated representative(s). Trainers will be experienced Garage Floor Coating employees and its affiliates.

You must complete the initial training program to our satisfaction and receive a training release certificate from your instructor before you begin Business operations. You must pay all expenses incurred during training, including travel, lodging and dining expenses and employees' salaries. We will provide you with all training materials at no additional charge. The training program includes instruction as outlined in the following chart. Each day will consist of at least six to eight hours of instruction. We may offer additional training programs and/or refresher courses, however, you are not required to attend such training.

Initial Training Schedule

SUBJECT	INSTRUCTOR	CLASSROOM HOURS	ONSITE HOURS
Getting Started	Thad Flores	1	0
Trailer and Equipment Set up and Operation	Fernando Fernandez	1	5
Floor Preparation and Coating Techniques	Fernando Fernandez	20	20
Warranty Issues and Management	Karlene Blair	2	0
Job Estimating	David Isho	2	3
Materials Purchasing	Joyce Chmura	1	0
Computer Setup and Operation	David Isho	3	0
Wireless Technology Training	Michael Maras	1	0
Employee Hiring	Mary Sorensen	1	0
Employee Training	Fernando Fernandez	1	0
Banking Transactions	Diane Everhart	1	0
Accounting Systems	Scott Lopez	2	0
Marketing Programs	Rob Hanson	1	0
Franchise Marketing and Networking	Rob Hanson	2	0
Customer Service	Rob Hanson	1	0
Business Issues and Ethics	Rob Hanson	1	0
Report Generation	David Isho	1	0
Outside Sales	David Isho	1	1
Other Topics	Rob Hanson	2	2
General Questions	Rob Hanson	2	2

Advertising

We will administer and execute a continuous local advertising campaign for the promotion of your Business or a group of Business in your region. The advertising is prepared by us, and by outside sources, and we use a variety of advertising media at our sole discretion. We will use the Local Advertising and Administration Fee paid by you each month to fund and support this advertising. If we do not spend all contributions by the end of each month, the funds will be carried forward into future months, but if we do not spend all contributions by the end of the 12th month from the month in which they were contributed, the funds will be refunded by pro rata share to the contributing Business(s).

We may establish a national advertising fund ("National Fund") for the common benefit of System franchisees. We may, in our sole discretion, also establish regional advertising funds ("Regional Fund(s)") for the benefit of System franchisees, whose Business are located within designated regions. We have the right to require you to participate in and contribute monthly to either or both the National Fund and/or Regional Fund which encompasses your Territory, a total amount not to exceed 1% of your monthly Sales in the manner we prescribe. We have the right to use National and Regional Fund contributions, in our sole discretion, to develop, produce, and distribute national, regional and/or local advertising and to create advertising and public relations materials which promote, in our sole judgment, the services offered by System franchisees, or those System franchisees whose businesses are located within the region for which the Regional Fund was established, as applicable. We have the right to require that advertising cooperatives be formed, changed, dissolved or merged.

If we establish a National Fund, we may require all System franchisees to contribute up to 1% of their monthly Sales to the National Fund. We may use these National Fund contributions to develop and prepare advertising that we distribute to System franchisees for their placement in the local media. The advertising is prepared by us and by outside sources. If we do not spend all fund contributions by the end of each fiscal year, the funds may be carried forward into the next fiscal year.

We do not receive payments (other than reimbursement for expenses) for administering the National Fund. We do not anticipate that any part of the fund contributions will be used for advertising that is principally a solicitation for the sale of additional franchises, but we reserve the right to include a notation in any advertisement indicating "Franchises Available." Although we anticipate that all advertising contributions will be spent in the fiscal year in which they accrue, any remaining amounts will be carried over to be expended during the next fiscal year.

We have the sole right to determine contributions and expenditures from the National Fund or any Regional Fund, or any other advertising program, and sole authority to determine the selection of the advertising materials and programs; provided, however, that we will make a good faith effort to expend these funds in the general best interests of the System on a national, regional or local basis. We are not required, under the Franchise Agreement, to spend any amount of National Fund contributions in your Territory and not all System franchisees will benefit directly or on a pro rata basis from our expenditures. Business owned by DCI may benefit directly or indirectly from national, regional or local advertising programs. We have the right to reimburse ourselves from National or Regional Fund contributions for reasonable costs and overhead, if any, as we may incur in activities which are reasonably related to directing and implementing the National or Regional Fund and advertising programs for franchisees and the System, including costs of personnel for creating and implementing advertising, promotional and marketing programs. There is no requirement that the National or any Regional Fund be audited. Upon your written request, we will provide you with an un-audited accounting of National or Regional Fund expenditures. Franchisees participating in the National Fund or in any Regional Fund will contribute to the fund at varying rates.

We or our designated entity may receive payment from Suppliers and other parties based in part on the purchase of Merchandise and Equipment by you through us or our designated entity, such payments being specifically referred to as cooperative fees. We may use the cooperative fees to advertise your Business, though we have no obligation to spend any amount of the cooperative fees in your Territory and not all System franchisees will benefit directly or on a pro rata basis from our expenditures.

We will maintain an Internet Website for Garage Floor Coating franchisees that will include a zip locator and a link to your personal Garage Floor Coating Franchise Website (your "Sitelet") that will be developed by a designated or approved supplier. Your Sitelet will include such information about your Business that we deem appropriate. We have the sole discretion to modify the content of and/or discontinue such Website at any time.

Site Selection and Opening

You are granted a license to operate a single Business in a specific territory mutually agreed upon by you and us. We, or our designee, will review proposed sites for the location of your Business; however, neither our review and/or acceptance of a site will constitute a representation or guaranty that your Business location will be successful. We will either approve or disapprove your proposed site within a reasonable time frame and will not withhold acceptance if the site meets our standards. It is solely your responsibility to obtain a mutually acceptable site (see Item 12 of this Offering Circular). We anticipate that you will open your Garage Floor Coating Business within two to three months from the date we sign the Franchise Agreement. The actual length of this period will depend, however, upon several factors, including, state licensing requirements, your ability to obtain a mutually acceptable site and the lease for that site, acceptable financing arrangements, the amount of necessary construction, build-out time, training schedules, delivery schedules for inventory and equipment, and other factors. We may require certain lease provisions. You may not sign a lease, modification or amendment without our prior written consent. Additionally, you must provide us with a copy of the signed lease within 10 days after it is signed. You must commence operations under the Franchise Agreement within 160 days from the date we sign the Franchise Agreement. If you fail to begin operating your Business within this period, we have the right to terminate the Franchise Agreement.

ITEM 12: TERRITORY

You will operate a single Business within a specific territory identified in the Franchise Agreement Your designated territory will be identified in an exhibit to your franchise agreement. The boundaries of your territory will coincide with the boundaries of 1 or more adjacent zip codes. In determining the zip codes for a territory, we will consider "qualified households". Definition of qualified household(s) may vary based on specific geographic locations. You will be permitted to engage in direct advertising and solicitation of clients only within the boundaries of your territory.

During the term of the Franchise Agreement, if you are in compliance with the Franchise Agreement, we will neither establish nor operate nor license another to establish or operate a Garage Floor Coating Business using the Proprietary Marks and System within the territory zip codes assigned to your business. For the purposes of sales credit and customer acceptance, you are obligated to verify that any coating services or repair services are performed only within the zip code boundaries of your Territory. We have the right to charge you, and if applicable credit the appropriate franchisee for any service revenue derived from services performed outside your assigned territory boundaries. The protection afforded under this paragraph relates solely to the operation of a Garage Floor Coating Business. We retain all other rights. Specifically, but not exclusively, we and/or our affiliates, licensees or designees, have the right to: (i) operate and license others the right to operate Garage Floor Coating Business using the Proprietary Marks and System outside the Territory; (ii) distribute products and services, now existing or developed in the future, in your Territory in the manner and through the channels of distribution as we, in our sole discretion, will determine.

We have not established any other franchises or company owned outlets or other channels of distribution for selling or offering similar products or services under a different trademark. Although the Franchise Agreement does not prohibit us from establishing these outlets or channels of distribution, we have no present plans to do so.

After you have been open for business for 6 full calendar months, for each subsequent six-month period, you must average a minimum of 50 floor coating projects in order to maintain your rights in the exclusive. If you fail to achieve this minimum sales quota, you will have one six-month probationary period immediately following the default to achieve the sales minimum. If you failure to achieve the sales minimum during the probationary period your exclusivity in the Territory will automatically and permanently terminate and we may, at any time after that, establish, operate or enfranchise additional Garage Floor Coating Business in your Territory.

ITEM 13: TRADEMARKS

Dexter Coatings, Inc., an Arizona corporation that is owned by certain of our principals, filed an application for registration of the following Marks identified below on the Principal Register at the United States Patent and Trademark Office:

MARK	SERIAL NUMBER	APPLICATION DATE
GARAGE FLOOR COATING FRANCHISE SYSTEM (word mark)	77025466	October 19, 2006
GARAGE FLOOR COATING FRANCHISE SYSTEM AND DESIGN (shown on UFOC cover page)	77025466	October 19, 2006

We grant you the right to establish and operate one Business under the name "Garage Floor Coating Franchise System" We will defend you against any claim, demand or suit concerning your right to use the Proprietary Marks.

The applications were based on actual use of the Marks. By not having a Principal Register registration for the Marks, Garage Floor Coating Franchise System, Inc. does not have certain presumptive legal rights granted by a registration.

We grant you the right to operate a franchise under the name "Garage Floor Coating Franchise System" shown on the cover page of this Offering Circular and garagefloorcoating.com (which we do not have a Principal Register registration). We or our affiliates may apply for or adopt additional trademarks or service marks and those may be licensed to you during the term of the franchise relationship. By trademark, we mean trade names, trademarks, service marks, and logotypes used to identify your Garage Floor Coating franchise or the products or services it sells.

118

GARAGE FLOOR COATING FRANCHISE SYSTEM, INC. ("Service Mark")

("Commercial Symbol")

The Proprietary Marks are subject to periodic revision by us. You will be notified in advance of any change in the Proprietary Marks and given ample time to change the same in your Business.

You must follow our rules when you use the Proprietary Marks. **You may not use the Garage Floor Coating name as part of a corporate, partnership, Limited Liability Company or assumed name.** You must use the Proprietary Marks in conjunction with the symbol "SM" or "®" as applicable and you may not use them in connection with the offer or sale of any unauthorized products or in any other manner which we do not explicitly authorize in writing. We reserve the right to approve all signs, stationery, business cards, forms, and other materials and supplies bearing the Proprietary Marks. You must use the Proprietary Marks, including trade dress, color combinations, designs, symbols, and slogans, only in the manner and to the extent we specifically permit in the Franchise Agreement, the Operations Manual, or by our prior written consent. All advertising, publicity, signs, decorations, furnishings, equipment or other materials employing in any way the words "Garage Floor Coating" or any derivative thereof or any other Proprietary Mark must be submitted to us and approved before first publication or use. We will not unreasonably withhold our approval.

No Proprietary Mark is registered in any state and no application for any such state registration has been made. We are not aware of any superior prior rights or infringing uses that could materially affect your use of the Proprietary Marks in any state.

Except as described above, there is no agreement currently in effect which significantly limits our right to use or license the use of our Proprietary Marks in a manner material to the franchise. There are no currently effective determinations of the U.S. Patent and Trademark Office, Trademark Trial and Appeal Board, the trademark administrator of any state or any court, and no pending interference, opposition or cancellation proceeding nor litigation involving the Proprietary Marks.

Any and all goodwill associated with the Proprietary Marks, including any goodwill that may have arisen through your use of them benefits us or our affiliates exclusively. You must sign any necessary papers, documents and assurances and fully cooperate with us or any other System franchisee in securing all necessary and required consents of any state agency or legal authority to use or register any of the Proprietary Marks. You must promptly notify us of any infringement of, or challenge to, the Proprietary Marks, and we will, in our sole discretion, take such action as we deem appropriate. We will indemnify and hold you harmless from any suits, proceedings, demands, obligations, actions or claims, including costs and reasonable attorneys' fees, for any alleged infringement under federal or state trademark law arising solely from your use of the Proprietary Marks in accordance with the Franchise Agreement or as we otherwise direct in writing, if you have promptly notified us of the claim. If we undertake the defense or prosecution of any litigation pertaining to any of the Proprietary Marks, you must sign any documents and do acts and things as may, in our attorneys' opinion, be necessary to carry out the defense or prosecution.

Use of a Supplier's or Vendor's trademark is subject to the approval of each Organization.

119

ITEM 14: PATENTS, COPYRIGHTS AND PROPRIETARY INFORMATION

We do not own any registered patents or copyrights that are material to the franchise, however, we claim common law copyright and trade secret protection for many aspects of the franchise System, including the Operations Manual and other manuals, advertising and promotional material, and training materials and programs.

The Franchise Agreement provides that the Operations Manual, our trade secrets and copyrighted materials, methods and other techniques and know-how are our exclusive and confidential property that we provide to you in confidence ("Confidential Information"). You agree to use the Confidential Information only for the purposes and in the manner we authorize in writing, which use will inure exclusively to our benefit. Our trade secrets include certain operations systems, policies, procedures, systems, compilations of information, records, specifications, manuals, supplier information, customer information, financial information and other confidential information which we or our affiliates have developed for use in the operation of the Franchised Business. You may not contest our ownership of our trade secrets, methods or procedures or contest our right to register, use or license others to use any of our trade secrets, methods and procedures. You and your heirs, successors and assigns (including your partners, officers, directors, shareholders, and their respective heirs, successors and assigns) and your employees and their respective heirs, successors and assigns, are prohibited from using and/or disclosing any Confidential Information in any manner other than as we permit in writing. Under the terms of the Franchise Agreement, you must sign, and cause certain employees to sign, confidentiality agreements in a form prescribed by us.

ITEM 15: OBLIGATION TO PARTICIPATE IN
THE ACTUAL OPERATION OF THE FRANCHISED BUSINESS

We require that you personally supervise the Franchised Business unless we authorize otherwise in writing. You will be required to learn and perform all of the operations of the business. If you are not on the premises, a trained manager under your supervision must be engaged in active management of your Business while it is open for business. You and your on-premises manager(s), if you have any, cannot have an interest in or business relationship with any

Floor Coatings business competitor(s). The manager need not have an ownership interest in the Franchised Business. The manager must sign a written agreement to maintain confidentiality of the trade secrets described in Item 14 of this Offering Circular. Each individual who owns an interest in the franchise entity must sign the Franchise Agreement.

While you are a Garage Floor Coating franchisee, you must not become involved in any business engaged in the sale and application of floor coatings and/or the sale of related merchandise for sale by us ("Competing Business") or give access to our proprietary information to anyone in competition with us or who is about to enter into any activity competitive with us.

Under the terms of the Franchise Agreement, your principals, partners or members, as applicable, must sign a Personal Guaranty agreeing to be bound by the non-competition agreement, confidentiality requirements and all of the other terms and obligations contained in the Franchise Agreement.

ITEM 16: RESTRICTIONS ON WHAT THE FRANCHISEE MAY SELL

You must offer for sale in your Business all Merchandise and Products, and only that those, specified by us. You must purchase all of the Merchandise, Equipment, Parts and Chemicals used in your Business from DCI or another approved vendor as specified by us. You must offer and sell all Service and Merchandise that we prescribe and only the Service and Merchandise that we prescribe. You may not sell any product or render any service in connection with your Business that does not meet our standards and specifications. You must refrain from any deviation from our standards and specifications. We may, in our sole discretion, change the type of Merchandise and/or Service(s) that you may offer and sell in connection with your Business.

You must operate your business for at least those months, days and hours that we specify in the Operations Manual. Under the current requirement, which we may change in the future, your Business must be open for business a minimum of eight (8) hours a day from Monday through Friday, and weekends as required by customer demands. Pets will not be allowed in the Business during business hours.

120

ITEM 17: RENEWAL, TERMINATION, TRANSFER AND DISPUTE RESOLUTION

The table set forth below lists certain important provisions of the Franchise Agreement and related agreements pertaining to renewal, termination, transfer and dispute resolution. You should read these provisions in the agreements attached to this Offering Circular. The agreements describe these provisions more fully than does the summary in the table.

PROVISION	SECTION IN FRANCHISE AGREEMENT	SUMMARY
a. Term of franchise	Section 2.1	10 years
b. Renewal or extension of the term	Section 2.2	You can renew the Franchise Agreement for an unlimited number of additional successive ten-year terms, subject to the conditions described below
c. Requirements for you to renew or extend[1]	Section 2.2	Right to remain in possession of your Business; completed all required remodeling; are not in default of the Franchise Agreement or any other agreement; paid us a renewal fee Of $5,000; satisfied our qualification and training requirements; signed a release; signed a current Franchise Agreement
d. Termination by you	No provision	Not applicable
e. Termination by us without cause	No provision	Not applicable
f. Termination by us with cause[1]	Section 14	We can terminate the Franchise Agreement if you default
g. Cause defined: defaults that can be cured	Sections 14.3 and 14.4	You have 10 days to cure non-payment; failure to procure a site; failure to complete initial training; failure to personally

		participate in the day-to-day operation; failure to comply with standards and procedures; failure to maintain prescribed hours; adverse conduct; unauthorized transfer. You have 30 days to cure failure to comply with the Franchise Agreement or other agreements. You have 180 days to cure failure to meet the minimum sales quotas
h. Cause defined: defaults that cannot be cured[2]	Sections 14.1 and 14.2	Non-curable defaults: you are convicted of or plead guilty or no contest to a felony or take part in criminal misconduct; you commit fraud; you make any misrepresentation on your franchise application; two defaults in any twelve-month period; you sell or purchase any unapproved product; you breach any other agreement; you misuse the Proprietary Marks or disclose Confidential Information; you violate any health, safety or sanitation law or ordinance or regulation; your lease is terminated; you violate the restrictive covenant; you make any assignment for the benefit of creditors or file for bankruptcy; bankruptcy or reorganization proceedings are brought on your behalf; execution is begun against you; you are insolvent; or you abandon the business
i. Your obligations on termination or non-renewal	Section 15	Obligations include: cease all operation under the Franchise Agreement; pay all money owed; discontinue use of the Proprietary Marks; direct the transfer of your telephone number(s); return the Operations Manual and proprietary software; permit us to inspect your financial records within six months of termination; and comply with the post-termination covenants described below
j. Assignment of contract by us	Section 12.5	There are no restrictions on our right to assign
k. "Transfer" by you: definition	Section 12	A transfer requiring our prior written consent occurs if you form a legal entity to run your Franchised Business, or if you are a legal entity and you assign, sell, pledge or transfer any portion of your stock, (partnership interest or ownership interest) or increase the number of outstanding shares of your stock
l. Our approval of transfer by franchisee	Section 12	We must consent in writing; approval is subject to the conditions described below
m. Conditions for our approval of transfer	Section 12	(1) All of your monetary obligations have been satisfied; (2) you have cured all existing defaults; (3) you have signed a general release; (4) you have provided to us a copy of the signed purchase agreement; (5) the transferee meets our criteria; (6) the transferee signs our Franchise Agreement; (7) you pay us a $5,000 transfer fee; (8) the transferee completes our training program; and (9) you comply with the post-termination provisions described below
n. Our right of first refusal to acquire your business	Section 12.3.1	You must first offer to sell to us on the same terms and conditions offered by a third party

o. Our option to buy back your franchise	Section 13	We may repurchase your franchise at any time in accordance with these provisions: we will provide a 90-day notice; we will pay you a buyback fee equal to three times your most current year's business Gross Income, or three

		times the initial franchise fee or the then-current franchise fee, whichever is greater; we will reimburse you for your reasonable expenses associated with the repurchase; we will assume, at our option, ownership of the assets, lease, etc. necessary to continue operating the Franchised Business, and may, in our sole discretion, reimburse you for your cost of those assets; you must comply with the post-termination provisions of the Franchise Agreement
p. Your death or disability	Section 12.2	Your legal representative will have the right to continue the Franchised Business if certain conditions are met
q. Non-competition covenants during the term of the Franchise Agreement	Section 16.1	No involvement in any competing business
r. Non-competition covenants after the Franchise Agreement is terminated or expires	Section 16.2	For a period of two (2) years, you and your family may not have any interest in any other similar business and/or company within 100 miles of the Territory or any other Territory licensed by us. For a period of two years you may not solicit business from customers of your former business nor solicit any employees of ours. For a period of two years you may not enter into any business granting franchises or licenses similar to our franchises
s. Modification of the Franchise Agreement	Section 22.1	The Franchise Agreement may only be changed by a written document signed by you and us
t. Integration or merger clause	Section 22.1	The Franchise Agreement constitutes the entire agreement by the parties; any other promises may not be enforceable
u. Dispute resolution by arbitration or mediation	Section 17	At our option, all disputes must be submitted first to mediation, in Arizona, otherwise disputes will be settled by arbitration in Phoenix, Arizona
v. Choice of forum	Section 17.1 and 17.3	Litigation in the State of Arizona, as permitted by state law (see the state-specific addenda attached to this Offering Circular)
w. Choice of law	Section 17.1	Arizona law applies, as permitted by state law (see the state-specific addenda attached to this Offering Circular). This choice of law should not be considered a waiver of any right conferred upon the Franchisor or upon the Franchisee by article 33 of the general business law of the state of New York

Note 1: These states have statutes which may supersede your Franchise Agreement in your relationship with us including the areas of termination and renewal of your franchise: ARKANSAS [Stat. Section 70-807], CALIFORNIA [Bus. & Prof. Code Sections 20000-20043], CONNECTICUT [Gen. Stat. Section 42-133e et seq.], DELAWARE [Code, tit.], HAWAII [Rev. Stat. Section 482E-1], ILLINOIS [815 ILCS 705/19 and 705/20], INDIANA [Stat. Section 23-2-2.7], IOWA [Code Sections 523H.1-523H.17], MICHIGAN [Stat. Section 19.854(27)], MINNESOTA [Stat. Section 80C.14], MISSISSIPPI [Code Section 75-24-51], MISSOURI [Stat. Section 407.400], NEBRASKA [Rev. Stat. Section 87-401], NEW JERSEY [Stat. Section 56:10-1], SOUTH DAKOTA [Codified Laws Section 37-5A-51], VIRGINIA [Code 13.1-557-574-13.1-564], WASHINGTON [Code Section 19.100.180], WISCONSIN [Stat. Section 135.03]. These and other states may have court decisions, which may supersede your franchise in your relationship with GARAGE FLOOR COATING FRANCHISE SYSTEM, INC., including the areas of termination and renewal of your franchise.

Note 2: A provision in the Franchise Agreement that provides for termination upon your bankruptcy may not be enforceable under federal bankruptcy law (11 U.S.C. Section 101 et seq.).

ITEM 18: PUBLIC FIGURES

We do not use any public figure to promote our franchises.

ITEM 19: EARNINGS CLAIMS

We do not furnish or authorize our salespeople to furnish any verbal or written information concerning the actual or potential sales, costs, income or profits of a Garage Floor Coating franchise. Actual results may vary from unit to unit and we cannot estimate the results of any particular Business.

Prospective franchisees should disregard any unauthorized information, whether verbal or written, concerning the actual, average, projected, forecasted or potential sales, costs, earnings or profits, or the prospects or chances of success, or representation or estimated dollar figures as to a franchisee's operation furnished by any person. A prospective franchisee should immediately notify us of any such unauthorized information or representation.

We encourage prospective franchisees to make their own independent investigation to determine whether or not the franchise may be profitable, and to consult with an attorney, existing franchisees, and other advisors before purchasing a Garage Floor Coating franchise. Actual results vary from franchise to franchise, and we cannot estimate the results of a particular franchise. Gross revenue and gross profit figures are affected by the actual market price of the Service and Merchandise offered by each franchisee. The actual market price for Service and Merchandise offered by a franchisee may vary according to the geographic location of the franchised Business and the concentration of competitors in the market. We have not conducted an investigation concerning the degree of impact, if any, that geographic location or any other variable may have on a particular Business's gross revenue or gross profit. Prospective franchisees should be aware of local market conditions before purchasing a franchise for a specific location.

ITEM 20: LIST OF OUTLETS

Franchised Business Status Summary

As of the date of this Offering Circular, there are no System franchises. As of the date of this Offering Circular, there are two Business locations owned by DCI. As of the date of this Offering Circular, there are no projected franchise openings.

Since the date of our inception through the date of this Offering Circular, we have never terminated, canceled, not renewed, or otherwise voluntarily or involuntarily ceased to do business with any franchisee, nor has any franchisee not communicated with us within the 10-week period immediately following the date of our inception. In the most recently completed fiscal year, we have not terminated any franchisee, nor has any franchisee canceled, not renewed, or otherwise voluntarily or involuntarily ceased to do business under the Franchise Agreement, nor has any Franchisee not communicated with us within 10 weeks following the application date. Our fiscal year ends December 31.

We provide the following estimates for openings of Garage Floor Coating franchises in the 2006 fiscal year:

STATE	FRANCHISE AGREEMENT SIGNED BUT OFFICE NOT OPENED	PROJECTED FRANCHISES DURING OUR NEXT FISCAL YEAR	PROJECTED OPENINGS IN THE NEXT FISCAL YEAR BY US OR OUR AFFILIATE
Arizona	0	2	2
Nevada	0	2	2
Texas	0	1	1
Georgia	0	1	1

Florida	0	1	1
TOTAL	**0**	**7**	**7**

ITEM 21: FINANCIAL STATEMENTS

Our financial statements listed below are attached as Exhibit 4.

• Unaudited Balance Sheet as of October 20, 2006.

ITEM 22: CONTRACTS

Included as Exhibits 5 and 6 to this Offering Circular are copies of all contracts or agreements proposed for use or in use regarding the offer of our franchise, including:

• The GARAGE FLOOR COATING FRANCHISE SYSTEM, INC. Franchise Agreement (Exhibit 5 to this Offering Circular)
• Personal Guaranty (Attachment B to the Franchise Agreement)
• Collateral Assignment of Lease (Attachment C to the Franchise Agreement)
• Conditional Assignment of your Telephone Numbers (Attachment D to the Franchise Agreement)
• Confidentiality and Restrictive Covenant Agreement (Attachment E to the Franchise Agreement)
• Confidentiality Agreement (Exhibit 6 to this Offering Circular)

ITEM 23: RECEIPT

124

Exhibit 10 of this Offering Circular contains a detachable document, in duplicate, acknowledging receipt of this Offering Circular by a prospective franchisee. You should sign both copies of the receipt. You should retain one signed copy for your records and return the other signed copy to: Mr. Rob Hanson, President & CEO, GARAGE FLOOR COATING FRANCHISE SYSTEM, INC., 3801 East Roeser Road, Suite #1, Phoenix, AZ 85040.

ABOUT THE AUTHOR

about the author

Ralph Massetti is President & CEO of The Franchise Builders, a franchise consulting, development, marketing and technology firm, with offices in Phoenix, Arizona and Boulder, Colorado. Aside from his experience and expertise as a Business and Franchise Consultant, he is a Certified Professional Search Engine Marketer and a candidate for the prestigious Certified Franchise Executive (CFE) designation.

Ralph is frequently sought out as an expert interviewee for franchise-related magazine and newspaper articles and a frequent contributor to trade publications. Ralph holds a Bachelor's Degree in Management as well as a Master's Degree in Business Administration and he served as founder and President of a prestigious publicly traded Internet firm. Ralph is also a licensed Private Pilot and when he's not helping new businesses achieve success through franchising, he enjoys getting a fresh perspective while soaring the skies.

Born and raised in Chicago, his true "hometown", Ralph and his family now live in the Boulder, Colorado area.

LaVergne, TN USA
29 October 2010
202794LV00007B/110/A